**INTRODUCING
ISSUES WITH
OPPOSING
VIEWPOINTS®**

Patriotism

Sabine Cherenfant, Book Editor

GREENHAVEN
PUBLISHING

Published in 2020 by Greenhaven Publishing, LLC
353 3rd Avenue, Suite 255, New York, NY 10010

Articles in Greenhaven Publishing anthologies are often edited for length to meet page requirements. In addition, original titles of these works are changed to clearly present the main thesis and to explicitly indicate the author's opinion. Every effort is made to ensure that Greenhaven Publishing accurately reflects the original intent of the authors. Every effort has been made to trace the owners of the copyrighted material.

Library of Congress Cataloging-in-Publication Data

Names: Cherenfant, Sabine, editor.
Title: Patriotism / Sabine Cherenfant, book editor.
Other titles: Patriotism (Greenhaven Publishing)
Description: First Edition. | New York : Greenhaven Publishing, 2020. | Series: Introducing issues with opposing viewpoints | Includes bibliographical references and index. | Audience: Grades 7–12.
Identifiers: LCCN 2019030946 | ISBN 9781534506657 (library binding) | ISBN 9781534506640 (paperback)
Subjects: LCSH: Patriotism—United States—Juvenile literature. | Nationalism—United States—Juvenile literature.
Classification: LCC JK1759 .P3554 2020 | DDC 323.6/50973—dc23
LC record available at https://lccn.loc.gov/2019030946

Manufactured in the United States of America

Website: http://greenhavenpublishing.com

Contents

Foreword   5

Introduction   7

Chapter 1: What Is Patriotism?

1. Americans Misunderstand Patriotism   12
   Michael Quirk
2. Nationalism Is a Significant Part of American Life   17
   Linton Weeks
3. Globalists and Nationalists Disagree on the Value of   24
   Patriotism
   Jonathan Haidt
4. What Is Chauvinism?   33
   Dave Wilton
5. Patriotism in the Face of War   37
   Patricia Pulham

Chapter 2: What Can Patriotism Do for a Country?

1. Global Patriotism Can Help Create a Better Future   43
   Marcel J. Harmon
2. What Role Does Patriotism Play in a Country's Struggle   49
   for Independence?
   Ma. Cielito Reyno
3. Patriotism Is Mandatory in Wartime   56
   Lumen Learning
4. How Americans Should View Patriotism in This Global   62
   Society
   Sharon L. Wisniewski
5. Impoverished Americans Still Believe in America   68
   Francesco Duina

Chapter 3: How Does Patriotism Relate to Current Issues?

1. Millennials and Patriotism   74
   Gabrielle Bosché
2. What Does Patriotism Mean in the US Today?   78
   Adam McCann

3. What Republicans and Democrats Believe Patriotism   86
    Means
    Kathy Frankovic
4. Marxism Is Not Un-American   90
    Bhaskar Sunkara
5. Nationalism and Hate   95
    Heidi Beirich
6. Athletes at the Center of the Patriotism Debate   103
    Anna De Fina

Facts About Patriotism   110
Organizations to Contact   112
For Further Reading   114
Index   117
Picture Credits   120

Foreword

Indulging in a wide spectrum of ideas, beliefs, and perspectives is a critical cornerstone of democracy. After all, it is often debates over differences of opinion, such as whether to legalize abortion, how to treat prisoners, or when to enact the death penalty, that shape our society and drive it forward. Such diversity of thought is frequently regarded as the hallmark of a healthy and civilized culture. As the Reverend Clifford Schutjer of the First Congregational Church in Mansfield, Ohio, declared in a 2001 sermon, "Surrounding oneself with only like-minded people, restricting what we listen to or read only to what we find agreeable is irresponsible. Refusing to entertain doubts once we make up our minds is a subtle but deadly form of arrogance." With this advice in mind, Introducing Issues with Opposing Viewpoints books aim to open readers' minds to the critically divergent views that comprise our world's most important debates.

Introducing Issues with Opposing Viewpoints simplifies for students the enormous and often overwhelming mass of material now available via print and electronic media. Collected in every volume is an array of opinions that captures the essence of a particular controversy or topic. Introducing Issues with Opposing Viewpoints books embody the spirit of nineteenth-century journalist Charles A. Dana's axiom: "Fight for your opinions, but do not believe that they contain the whole truth, or the only truth." Absorbing such contrasting opinions teaches students to analyze the strength of an argument and compare it to its opposition. From this process readers can inform and strengthen their own opinions, or be exposed to new information that will change their minds. Introducing Issues with Opposing Viewpoints is a mosaic of different voices. The authors are statesmen, pundits, academics, journalists, corporations, and ordinary people who have felt compelled to share their experiences and ideas in a public forum. Their words have been collected from newspapers, journals, books, speeches, interviews, and the Internet, the fastest growing body of opinionated material in the world.

Introducing Issues with Opposing Viewpoints shares many of the well-known features of its critically acclaimed parent series, Opposing

Viewpoints. The articles allow readers to absorb and compare divergent perspectives. Active reading questions preface each viewpoint, requiring the student to approach the material thoughtfully and carefully. Photographs, charts, and graphs supplement each article. A thorough introduction provides readers with crucial background on an issue. An annotated bibliography points the reader toward articles, books, and websites that contain additional information on the topic. An appendix of organizations to contact contains a wide variety of charities, nonprofit organizations, political groups, and private enterprises that each hold a position on the issue at hand. Finally, a comprehensive index allows readers to locate content quickly and efficiently.

Introducing Issues with Opposing Viewpoints is also significantly different from Opposing Viewpoints. As the series title implies, its presentation will help introduce students to the concept of opposing viewpoints and learn to use this material to aid in critical writing and debate. The series' four-color, accessible format makes the books attractive and inviting to readers of all levels. In addition, each viewpoint has been carefully edited to maximize a reader's understanding of the content. Short but thorough viewpoints capture the essence of an argument. A substantial, thought-provoking essay question placed at the end of each viewpoint asks the student to further investigate the issues raised in the viewpoint, compare and contrast two authors' arguments, or consider how one might go about forming an opinion on the topic at hand. Each viewpoint contains sidebars that include at-a-glance information and handy statistics. A Facts About section located in the back of the book further supplies students with relevant facts and figures.

Following in the tradition of the Opposing Viewpoints series, Greenhaven Publishing continues to provide readers with invaluable exposure to the controversial issues that shape our world. As John Stuart Mill once wrote: "The only way in which a human being can make some approach to knowing the whole of a subject is by hearing what can be said about it by persons of every variety of opinion and studying all modes in which it can be looked at by every character of mind. No wise man ever acquired his wisdom in any mode but this." It is to this principle that Introducing Issues with Opposing Viewpoints books are dedicated.

Introduction

"What greater expression of faith in the American experiment than this, what greater form of patriotism is there than the belief that America is not yet finished, that we are strong enough to be self-critical, that each successive generation can look upon our imperfections and decide that it is in our power to remake this nation to more closely align with our highest ideals?"[1]

-Former US President Barack Obama

In his 2015 speech marking the fiftieth anniversary of the civil rights march in Selma, Alabama, then-President Barack Obama issued a response to right-wing criticism of his refusal to use the term "radical Islamic terrorists" when discussing terrorist attacks—a decision that they deemed unpatriotic.[1] The quote above from this speech highlights an issue that has been at the forefront of current social frictions, such as questions of immigration, political inclinations, and race relations. What is patriotism? How do we define patriotic and unpatriotic behaviors, and how do we measure our peers' level of patriotism?

Since 2016, with the election of Donald Trump as president of the United States, a lot has changed. "Make America Great Again" (MAGA) was the slogan for Donald Trump's presidential campaign. When he won the election, journalists—especially those who were previously skeptical or dismissive of him—scrambled to understand what in his message had drawn the majority of the public toward him. It is true that when referring to the 2016 presidential election and to the Trump presidency nationalism must be considered, but understanding what Americans who describe themselves as patriotic value is important to understanding what the public currently prioritizes in American politics. Patriotism—though often entwined with nationalism—is its own distinct quality. At the core of current issues seems to be this longing for a stronger sense of patriotism, which is what President Donald Trump leveraged in his campaign. It is why this topic is relevant now more than ever.

Andrea Baumeister of the *Encyclopedia Britannica* defines patriotism as the "feeling of attachment and commitment to a country, nation, or political community."[2] The term itself refers to a healthy attachment to one's country, which is why it should not be confused with nationalism. Colton Carpenter of the *Harvard Political Review* explains that nationalism "entails loyalty to a nation, a group of people who share a racial origin and characteristics, language, customs, geography, history, and government."[3] Many times, this loyalty develops into ethnocentrism and a sense of superiority that, in turn, leads to unfortunate events. A prime example would be the 2015 Charleston church shooting, in which the shooter was a white supremacist.[4]

The term "chauvinism" traditionally refers to patriotism driven to the extreme. It is the eponym of Nicholas Chauvin, a soldier under Napoleon Bonaparte (Emperor of the French, 1804-1814) who was unwaveringly loyal to him even after Bonaparte was recognized as a controversial figure.[5] The concept of following a set of beliefs blindly in the name of patriotism is not new and is unto itself part of what characterizes the misconception about patriotism. Events like the Holocaust of 1941 to 1945, the Rwanda genocide of 1994, and the 1937 Parsley massacre of Haitians living in the Dominican Republic were also incited by skewed understandings of patriotism and national identity.

Initially, patriotism was considered an essential quality for a country to function. Vicki Simmons of the *New Patriot Journal* traces its importance back to the beginning of civilization, emphasizing how it helped humanity maintain its existence. She adds that it is patriotism that essentially unifies a country, since the sense of responsibility that a citizen feels for fellow citizens—which pushes her to reach out to those in need and to sacrifice herself for the greater good of the community—is a devotion to the republic.[6] Patriotism also relates to civic obligations like paying taxes, performing jury duty, engaging in charity, and voting. All these factors play into the administration of a country.

However, what patriotism means and how it's demonstrated varies based on social status, race, ethnicity, and religion. According to Joan C. Williams of the *Los Angeles Times*, working-class white Americans are considered the most patriotic of all groups, placing a high value on the military and on patriotic symbolism like the flag. Williams concludes this from the fact that most Americans who join the military are from the middle class and working class. Many times, they join because of the incentives the military offers. It alleviates the financial burden of going to college and receiving good health-care—something the upper class do not have to worry about.[7] With that being said, it is important to note that marginalized groups, who more often tend to fall in the working-class category, struggle with what is determined to be acceptable expressions and attitudes toward patriotism. At times, the attitudes and actions of marginalized groups can collide with what most Americans accept as patriotic.

In 2012, comedian Chris Rock angered many Americans by coining the Fourth of July as "white peoples independence day [*sic*]," which flared allegations of a lack of patriotism on his part.[8] This debate over what the United States represents to non-white and otherwise marginalized citizens culminated with NFL player Colin Kaepernick's taking-a-knee protest during the singing of the national anthem at NFL games, which began in 2016. He wanted to raise awareness of the disproportional number of killings of unarmed black citizens by police officers in the United States. It spurred a national debate over whether it is right to express disagreement over national issues by challenging established proper conducts of patriotism, such as reciting the Pledge of Allegiance and standing up for the singing of the national anthem. This also brings to mind questions surrounding the burning of the flag by American protesters. Though the Supreme Court ruled in 1989 that flag burning is protected as a form of symbolic speech, it remains a highly controversial form of protest. The question remains: can these instances be singled out as particular acts of despair, or do they attest to a blatant disregard for the country as a whole? Could acts of protest be considered patriotic for their role in encouraging the betterment of a country?

Understanding the role of patriotism in building a country, along with analyzing the rough edges of a topic that can occasionally be a sensitive one, is the focus of *Introducing Issues with Opposing Viewpoints: Patriotism*. By reading different viewpoints on patriotism, learning about the various practices related to it like chauvinism, Marxism, and nationalism, and exploring its role in different social groups, students will get a chance to form their own opinions on what it means to be patriotic and the ways in which this value might be challenged.

Notes

1. Nancy Letourneau, "Barack Obama's Most Important Speech," *Washington Monthly*, February 19, 2019. https://washingtonmonthly.com/2019/02/19/barack-obamas-most-important-speech/.
2. Andrea Baumeister, "Patriotism," *Encyclopedia Britannica*, May 4, 2016. https://www.britannica.com/topic/patriotism-sociology.
3. Colton Carpenter, "Choosing Patriotism over Nationalism," *Harvard Political Review*, April 1, 2019. https://harvardpolitics.com/columns-old/patriotism-over-nationalism/
4. Rebecca Hersher, "'What Happened to You, Dylann?' Victim's Friend Asks Roof At Sentencing," NPR, January 11, 2017. https://www.npr.org/sections/thetwo-way/2017/01/11/509299574/what-happened-to-you-dylann-victims-friend-asks-roof-at-sentencing
5. "Chauvinism," *Encyclopedia Britannica*, July 11, 2002. https://www.britannica.com/topic/chauvinism.
6. Vicki Simmons, "5 Reasons why Patriotism is Important," *New Patriot Journal*, January 8, 2018. http://newpatriotjournal.com/Articles/Puerto_Ricos_Nuclear_Option_Statehood_Strategy
7. Joan C. Williams, "Even on July 4, the Working Class and the Elites Don't See Eye to Eye," *Los Angeles Times*, July 4, 2017. https://www.latimes.com/opinion/op-ed/la-oe-williams-patriotism-and-the-white-working-class-20170704-story.html.
8. Gael F. Cooper, "Chris Rock Draws Fire for July 4 Tweet about 'white peoples independence day'," Today, July 5, 2012. https://www.today.com/news/chris-rock-draws-fire-july-4-tweet-about-white-peoples-863832.

Chapter 1

What Is Patriotism?

Reciting the Pledge of Allegience is required in schools in forty-six US states.

Americans Misunderstand Patriotism

Michael Quirk

"A patriotism that does not reflexively exclude 'the other' as a kind of unpatriotic cancer on the body politic is manifestly preferable to one that does so as a matter of dogma."

During the 2016 presidential election, the United States witnessed two kinds of patriotic rhetoric. One of them focused on hostility and "us versus them," the other focused on a broader "we." Yet Michael Quirk writes in this excerpted viewpoint that both were problematic. Both focused on how great the United States was and continues to be, and how exceptional they want the country to remain in the future. Nevertheless, Quirk argues that this is not what patriotism really is. Patriotism is a stubborn love for a country simply because it is your own country. It has nothing to do with a country's military power and with how exceptional or great a country appears to be. Michael Quirk is an information technology manager at the New School in New York.

"Patriotism, Nationalism, Exceptionalism," by Michael Quirk, The Editorial Board of Public Seminar, August 1, 2016. Reprinted by permission.

AS YOU READ, CONSIDER THE FOLLOWING QUESTIONS:
1. What did Michael Quirk point out as the key differences between the 2016 presidential campaigns of President Donald Trump and former Secretary of State Hillary Clinton?
2. What event led the author to understand what he considers to be the real meaning of patriotism?
3. What reaction did the author assert would have been more appropriate at the baseball game where they announced the death of Osama Bin Laden?

O ver the past fortnight, two very different versions of patriotism were put on display. One of them was xenophobic, hostile, and downright plug-ugly. The other was hopeful, inclusive, and cheerful. Even though the media-saturated presentations of each were designed to "sell" a prepackaged vision of the political community known as The United States of America, and as such should be taken with a grain of salt and *caveat emptor* in the back of one's mind at all times, it is clear to me which one of the two is morally and politically superior. The Republican candidate's speech was framed in the first person singular, peppered with the pronoun "I" (except when the candidate referred to himself, as is his wont, in the third person as "Donald Trump," an idiosyncrasy that I find chillingly disconcerting). The Democratic candidate spoke in the first person plural, as part of a wider "we." Enough said, even if one might be granted a certain skepticism about whether Hillary Clinton will make good on her reference to a wider "we." A patriotism that does not reflexively exclude "the other" as a kind of unpatriotic cancer on the body politic is manifestly preferable to one that does so as a matter of dogma.

Yet both visions share something that I find troubling. I suspect that both rest on an identification of American patriotism with "greatness," one pledging to "Make America great again" and to recover this lost greatness, the other proclaiming that "America was always great and is great now," and to continue and expand that greatness. Aside from the vagueness and slipperiness of the term "great," I think that both kinds of rhetoric miss the point. Two stories explain why I think so.

The Haitian flag flies above the wreckage of the Presidential Palace in Port-au-Prince, Haiti, after the devastating earthquake of 2010.

A few years back, I was teaching and doing random I.T. work at a high school in Brooklyn. Many students were of Afro-Caribbean descent. In 2010 an earthquake of 7.0 magnitude struck Haiti, with an epicenter just outside Port-au-Prince, its capital city with a population of close to 1 million people. The devastation was unimaginable. The death toll was between 100,000 to 160,000 souls. Collapsed buildings, destroyed infrastructure, mass graves — all were elements of the horror. The morning after, the school's population was addressed by a Haitian colleague, a history teacher, who had family in Haiti (all survived). He spoke Kreyol to the students — despite my shaky French, I could really only decipher a word here and there, but his somber tones conveyed the point.

It was then that I understood what "patriotism" meant, as well as how, why, and under what conditions it could be a virtue.

Apart from its heart-stirring beginnings with Toussaint L'Ouverture's slave revolt, the history of Haiti has lurched from one heart-rending catastrophe to another, whether natural as in the case of the earthquake or political as in the case of the barbaric reign of the Duvaliers. It is a sad history that would dishearten anyone. Yet my colleague exuded what can only be understood as a keen, steadfast love of Haiti through his sadness. That love was palpable. And the love had nothing to do with visions of Haitian grandeur. He loved Haiti because he was Haitian. He loved his country Haiti, and mourned its losses, because it was his.

Another event convinced me that many Americans, perhaps even most, mistake patriotism for a false simulacrum, an expression of nationalism, of exceptionalism, of unalloyed righteousness and majesty. It expresses a conviction that The United States of America is worth loving because, maybe *only* because, it is great beyond measure. On May 2, 2011, I was watching a baseball game on television (for me, the only sport that matters). It was probably the Mets (for me, the team that matters most), but I forget whether it actually was the Mets or not, or what city in which the game was played. I do vividly recall this: the announcer at the game suddenly proclaimed, jumbo-tron aflame with pictures, that Osama Bin Laden had been assassinated in Abbotabad, Pakistan, by a group of Navy Seals. The crowd immediately cheered in applause, and then, with one voice, started to loudly chant "USA! USA!"

A chill ran up my spine, but not because I was particularly disturbed by the actions of the Navy Seals. Osama Bin Laden was a mass-murderer by any standard, and whether the actual assassination was morally justified or permissible under the standards of international law (I have my doubts), he was not the kind of person whose demise was to be regretted. What bothered me was the "USA! USA!" Acts of war may, under certain circumstances, be permissible or even obligatory. Their results, when successful, may be occasion for relief and even thanksgiving. But the assassination of the Al Qaida chieftain was not, on any understanding, analogous to the Mets winning the National League pennant. That was what the reaction of the crowd sounded like. "USA! USA!" is a sports victory chant, like "Number 1! Number 1!" It is fitting to use it when the US Soccer team clinches an Olympic medal. But in these circumstances a more somber, even solemn reaction was called for. That one's native land might be "Number 1!" or a "great" military power, is not the point of a true love of country. There was more patriotism inherent in my single colleague's cry of anguish for his Haitian homeland than in a stadium full of baseball fans.

G.K. Chesterton once mocked the old cliché "My country right or wrong" as on a par with "My mother drunk or sober." But Chesterton's quip is double-edged. Someone who argues that one has to go along with anything the government of one's country establishes as policy, whether it is launching the Spanish-American war or any other moral or strategic disaster, is a bit like thinking "well, my mother is absolutely hammered, and wants to go drag racing on the freeway, but well, hey, she's my mother, so I will give her the keys to the car." You would be culpably wrong to do so. But that does not make her any less your mother. You will love her anyway — because she's yours, not because she is "great" whatever she does.

[…]

EVALUATING THE AUTHOR'S ARGUMENTS:

In the viewpoint, the author argues that patriotism in the United States is too often tied with greatness. Why do you think the author believes this to be an issue? Quirk also supported his argument with two anecdotes. Do you feel like the anecdotes sufficiently back up his argument? Why or why not?

Viewpoint

2

Nationalism Is a Significant Part of American Life

Linton Weeks

"Call it what you will — American nationalism or patriotism — it is covering the country like a Wi-Fi cloud — above the fruited plain from sea to shining sea."

As this viewpoint explains, nationalism is ingrained in American culture and rhetoric, announcing itself through political campaigns, sports events, and national holidays. Whether it is a positive aspect of American life is debatable. On one hand, it promotes a sense of community and strengthens every citizen's sense of identity and belonging. On the other hand, it gives rise to a sense of superiority toward other groups, and it sometimes alienates Americans from other countries and nations. To show how nationalism sustains American politics, Linton Weeks examines quotes from former presidential candidates Sarah Palin, Rick Perry, and Mitt Romney, as well as former Vice President Joe Biden, in which they cast people whose attitudes do not align with their beliefs as unpatriotic. Additionally, patriotism and nationalism can help in sustaining businesses—think of how well "made in America" products sell. Linton Weeks is a reporter who has written for the *Washington Post* and NPR.

1. What are some nationalistic or patriotic practices and expressions displayed at sport events?
2. What is onr example provided in this viewpoint of a time when a politician has used patriotic rhetoric to support a speech?
3. According to this viewpoint, how do businesses like Made in USA Forever use patriotism to attract consumers?

Picture this: An alternate-reality, suspended-in-space American metropolis where steampunk contraptions — like propeller-driven dirigibles, squeaky trolley wires and clunky robotic creatures — operate against a backdrop of clanging liberty bells; red, white and blue powder kegs; and jingoistic posters warning: "Patriots! Arm Thyself Against the Foreigners and Anarchists!"

OK. So you can't quite picture it. No sweat. It's the surrealistic setting of *Bioshock: Infinite*, a video game—sequel to the critically acclaimed *Bioshock*—scheduled for release from Irrational Games in 2012.

The storyline is imaginative, assimilating eclectic influences. But one salient characteristic is unmistakable: The pro-Uncle Sam, protectionist feel of the game reflects the mood of many present-day American nationalists.

"The nationalism thrown throughout this is so overt," says video game critic Hilary Goldstein in a preview trailer.

You don't need to fire up the Xbox 360 to know that there has been among many Americans a swell of nationalism in the years following the Sept. 11, 2001, attacks.

- Go to a baseball game where fans often croon "God Bless America" during the seventh-inning stretch.
- Check out the American flag pins on the lapels or collars of nearly every politician.
- Listen to Toby Keith's current hit *Made in America* and read how it inspired a Michigan kindergarten class to create an "American-made show-and-tell."

Many companies use "Made in the USA" labels as a marketing tactic to tap into consumers' sense of patriotism or nationalism.

Call it what you will—American nationalism or patriotism—it is covering the country like a Wi-Fi cloud—above the fruited plain from sea to shining sea.

Where does this rising nationalism spring from? And is it a positive or a negative trait for a country? That all depends ...

A Sense of Selfhood

Nationalism flows through our lives every day, observes Lloyd Kramer, author of the recent book *Nationalism in Europe and America*.

And, like most "isms," Kramer says, nationalism carries with it both good and bad characteristics. "When people feel committed to larger communities or interests or to ideas of human rights and political progress, for example, nationalism can contribute to a sense of hope about the future. It can build positive personal and collective identities and a sense of selfhood in the modern world."

On the other hand, he says, "nationalism often encourages fears of all kinds of other people: fears of other religions or races or cultures or ethnic groups or homosexuals. This fear can be mobilized for violence and scapegoating. It can lead people to feel aggrieved and constantly at risk."

In various ways, he adds, "nationalism can contribute to human progress and freedom and education and economic vitality, or it can contribute to violence, fear and international conflicts."

Nationalism, according to Kramer, is often in full flower on national holidays, during major sports events and at public memorials for deceased military troops. And nationalistic symbols, rituals and rhetoric are especially ramped up as the country moves toward a presidential election.

A Political Tool?

He's not kidding.

Patriotism permeates contemporary American politics. As do accusations of unpatriotic behavior. Of course, the word "patriot" is a subjective characterization, and most politicians use it as code for someone who shares their beliefs.

Americans "are a patriotic people," said Mitt Romney at the recent Republican presidential debate in Orlando. "We place our hand over our heart during the playing of the national anthem. No other people on Earth do that." So does that mean that people who don't place their hands over their hearts while the anthem is played are not patriots?

Speaking to a Tea Party gathering in New Hampshire on Labor Day weekend, possible presidential candidate Sarah Palin said, "We patriots should not focus on petty political squabbles and media game sound bites. The Tea Party has got to be focused on the broader, much more important goals of this movement—replace Obama." Does that mean that someone who supports the president of the United States is not a patriot?

From the Democratic angle, Texas Rep. Sheila Jackson Lee, speaking recently on the *Tavis Smiley Show*, suggested that members of the Tea Party should "stop being Tea Party people instead of patriots and Americans." Does that mean a Tea Partier cannot also be a patriot and an American?

And Rick Perry in a new Web ad intones, "We don't need a president who apologizes for America. I believe in America. I believe in her purpose and her promise. ... God bless the United States of America."

After watching that ad, CNN's Carol Costello asked: "Should patriotism be a political tool?" She then pointed out that "patriotism has worked for Democrats, too, during the 2008 campaign. Vice presidential candidate Joe Biden said wealthy Americans should pay more taxes because it's time to be patriotic."

The Patriotic Center

Patriotism, nationalism. Is there a difference?

Peter Rutland, a professor of government at Wesleyan University in Middletown, Conn., says that in the U.S., the word "nationalism" often has negative connotations. "So we talk instead about patriotism."

He says, "Other people are nationalists; we are patriots."

But for the sake of argument, the terms "nationalism" and "patriotism" are pretty much interchangeable, Rutland says. He studies this instinct on a global level and posts observations on his NationalismWatch blog.

Rutland, Kramer and others who track nationalism point out that U.S. nationalism has swelled since 2001. Countrywide concerns about a faltering economy and a flood of immigration only intensify the notion of nationalism.

Both liberal and conservative politicians have been adapting their language, Rutland says, "to try to appeal to the patriotic median voter."

Rutland says that in light of that quest for the patriotic center, Obama's language has been particularly striking. "If you read his speech announcing his candidacy in Springfield, Ill., or his inaugural address, you see a heavy emphasis on the common national narrative —the sacrifices of Gettysburg, the legacy of past generations, etc.— classic nationalist/patriotic imagery."

Shovels To Snowshoes

That nod toward nationalism served Obama well in the 2008 election.

It has also worked for a number of business people, such as Todd Lipscomb. Not too long ago, Lipscomb was an executive in a California tech company. He lived in and traveled through Asia and the Pacific Rim for seven years. As his American company's global business increased, Lipscomb began to worry about the folks—their jobs and financial futures— back in the U.S.

Four years ago, he resigned from his company, moved home to California and launched the website Made in USA Forever. He sells products—everything from shovels to snowshoes—that are domestically manufactured.

"Stand with us to protect America's ability to produce, create jobs, and remain a world leader," the website intones.

From his home in San Clemente, Lipscomb says "sales are surging. Conversely to the economic trends, the bad news has energized my customer base."

Customers know "they are doing something real for our economy," Lipscomb says. "Every item is made here from U.S.A. components, so from the farmer that grows the cotton through every step of the way it helps our economy and creates jobs in a virtuous circle."

There are many similar sites for domestically manufactured products, including Made in USA and the Made in America store.

Lipscomb's website offers more than 2,800 products from over 480 "mostly small, family-owned business," Lipscomb says. But he adds, "Where we are weak is in electronics."

Lipscomb has written a couple of books about his experience, including *Re-Made in America: How We Can Restore Jobs, Retool Manufacturing and Compete with the World*. The issue of nationalism or patriotism is not a partisan concern, he says. He has been asked to appear on Ed Shultz's progressive radio show as well as the conservative *Fox & Friends* national TV program.

He says his website attracts people of all stripes. "Conservatives, progressives, outdoorsmen, union members, immigrants, and many, many other groups come together on the website as Americans."

In the end, he says, "this is not a red state or blue state issue, but truly a red, white and blue one."

EVALUATING THE AUTHOR'S ARGUMENTS:

In this viewpoint, Linton Weeks briefly quotes Carol Costello's pertinent question, "Should patriotism be a political tool?" Based on the viewpoint, what does the author seem to believe is the answer to this question? How would you answer this question? As you do so, consider the pros and cons of your argument.

Viewpoint 3

"Patriotism is...a commitment to a local and circumscribed group instead of adopting a universal or 'citizen of the world' identity."

Globalists and Nationalists Disagree on the Value of Patriotism

Jonathan Haidt

Globalists argue that patriotism puts people from other countries at risk. When people idolize their own country, it allows their leaders to attack other countries in the name of patriotism. Jonathan Haidt argues that although war is sometimes inevitable, having a globalist perspective on the world as opposed to a nationalist one allows leaders and citizens alike to solve conflicts with a humanistic approach. In this excerpted viewpoint, Jonathan Haidt highlights a pertinent argument against patriotism. As the author explains, the appeal of President Trump was his willingness to penalize "political correctness" and champion decisions that benefit Americans as opposed to global society. Jonathan Haidt is a professor in the Business and Society program at New York University's Stern School of Business.

"The Ethics of Globalism, Nationalism, and Patriotism," by Jonathan Haidt, Center for Humans & Nature, Fall 2016. Reprinted by permission. This essay was originally published in the Center's Minding Nature journal, a triennial online publication that explores the values and practices of democratic ecological citizenship. The original article publication can be found in the Center's Minding Nature's Fall 2016, Volume 9, Number 3 issue (https://www.humansandnature.org/the-ethics-of-globalism-nationalism-and-patriotism).

AS YOU READ, CONSIDER THE FOLLOWING QUESTIONS:

1. What does George Monbiot state as a pro and a con of patriotism in Britain in his essay titled "The New Chauvinism," according to this viewpoint?
2. What are the four values that philosopher David Miller believes should guide the immigration policies of liberal democracies?
3. What did *New York Times* columnist David Brooks recommend with respect to the globalist-nationalist debate, according to Haidt?

[...]

Given their fundamental disagreements over human nature and the moral value of parochialism, it is inevitable that Globalists and Nationalists would disagree about the moral value of patriotism.

Most definitions of patriotism refer to positive feelings about one's country (love, devotion, pride) and a sense of duty or obligation to support or protect it. Patriotism is therefore a form of parochialism—it is a commitment to a local and circumscribed group instead of adopting a universal or "citizen of the world" identity. This is why Globalists are often critical of patriotism, and why they sometimes say things about patriotism, or about their country, that Nationalists perceive to be disloyal at best, and treasonous at worst.

When a country is attacked by a foreign enemy, there is almost always a surge of patriotism. People have a strong urge to come together, and many of them reach for the flag. Americans saw this happen after the Japanese attack on Pearl Harbor, and again after the Al Qaeda attacks of September 11, 2001. Britain saw this happen at the start of both World Wars, and again after the Al Qaeda attacks on the London transport system in 2005. In the wake of those terrorist attacks, British intellectuals debated whether some form of patriotism was compatible with progressivism.

George Monbiot, a leading thinker of the British left, took a strong position against the moral value of patriotism. In an essay

The American flag is often considered a quintessential symbol of American patriotism and values. It tends to be displayed and treated with reverence.

titled "The New Chauvinism," Monbiot rejected what he called "an emerging national consensus," which included some left-of-center writers, that "what we need in Britain is a renewed sense of patriotism."[1] Monbiot granted that a widely shared sense of patriotism might make British citizens (including Muslim citizens) less likely to attack each other, but he made the good counter-point that patriotism makes the state more inclined to attack other countries, for it knows it is likely to command the support of its people. If patriotism were not such a powerful force in the United States, could Bush have invaded Iraq?

Monbiot then asserted that "internationalists" (i.e., globalists) should use a strictly utilitarian framework to resolve moral questions because internationalists believe that all lives are of equal worth. He then argued that from this utilitarian perspective, patriotism is almost always unethical:

> *When confronted with a conflict between the interests of your country and those of another, patriotism, by definition, demands that you should choose those of your own. Internationalism, by contrast, means choosing the option which delivers most good or least harm to people, regardless of where they live. It tells us that someone living in Kinshasa is of no less worth than someone living in Kensington, and that a policy which favours the interests of 100 British people at the expense of 101 Congolese is one we should not pursue. Patriotism, if it means anything, tells us we should favour the interests of the 100 British people. How do you reconcile this choice with liberalism? How, for that matter, do you distinguish it from racism?*

This is the kind of statement that turns many people away from Globalism. Most people believe that that their own government should place their welfare above that of foreigners, just as most people believe that their own spouse, mother, friend, boss, or teammate should care more about them than about a stranger far away. The willingness to erase local loyalties and obligations in order to maximize overall utility makes sense in John Lennon's imaginary world, but it is sacrilege from a Durkheimian perspective in which people have distinctive duties tied to their particular roles and relationships. And if Burke and Smith are correct, then universalism won't even deliver the benefits in reality that it promises in the abstract.

To be a nationalist, in America or in Europe, is to be frequently lectured to and called a rube by the globalist elite. The globalists assert things to be obvious and indisputable facts (e.g., "diversity is our strength") that seem to nationalists to be obvious and indisputable falsehoods. The globalists explain away the nationalists' policy preferences as resulting both from lack of education and from selfishness (i.e., not wanting immigrants taking scarce resources from the National Health Service). The globalists assemble panels of economists and other academics, and sometimes even movie stars, to argue their case. This is why Brexit leader Michael Gove said, "I think people in this country have had enough of experts." This is why Donald Trump's attacks on "political correctness" have won him the gratitude of so many working-class and rural white voters. Even if you are a globalist, can you see why nationalists are often full of seething resentment? Can you see why people who feel a deep emotional attachment to their country and want to preserve its sovereignty and culture are angry at people who tell them that they are wrong to do so?

So let us take another look at patriotism. Are there forms that might be acceptable to both globalists and to nationalists?

Patriotism Reconsidered

As the conflict between globalists and nationalists has moved to center stage in many countries in recent months, several commentators have offered insightful new thinking about patriotism and nationalism. The key question all have addressed is: how can people show love and loyalty to their nation in ways that bring benefits to their nation while minimizing the harm done both to immigrants within the country and to citizens of other countries?

The economist Larry Summers responded to the Brexit vote with an article titled: "Voters Deserve Responsible Nationalism not Reflex Globalism."[2] As an economist who is firmly convinced of the value of international trade, he acknowledged that big trade agreements, such as NAFTA, have often failed to live up to the hype that had been used to sell them to voters. He noted that "the willingness of people to be intimidated by experts into supporting cosmopolitan outcomes appears for the moment to have been exhausted." He urged Western nations to adopt a new approach that directly rejects Monbiot's universalism:

> *A new approach has to start from the idea that the basic responsibility of government is to maximise the welfare of citizens, not to pursue some abstract concept of the global good. . . . What is needed is a responsible nationalism—an approach where it is understood that countries are expected to pursue their citizens' economic welfare as a primary objective but where their ability to harm the interests of citizens elsewhere is circumscribed. International agreements would be judged not by how much is harmonised or by how many barriers are torn down but whether citizens are empowered.*

Examining immigration rather than trade, the philosopher David Miller just published a book with the timely title *Strangers in Our Midst*.[3] Like Summers, he concludes that states do have special duties to care for their own citizens, even as they attempt to act humanely toward others. In the end he recommends that the immigration policies of liberal democracies be guided by four values: weak cosmopolitanism, national self-determination, fairness, and social integration. By "weak cosmopolitanism" he means a broadly humanitarian orientation in which "we must always consider the effects of our actions on all those who will bear the consequences, no matter who they are or whether they are in any way connected to us," yet at the same time, he believes we are not obligated to treat the claims and interests of non-citizens as equal to those of citizens. Miller specifically rejects as overly demanding and unrealistic a "strong cosmopolitanism" in which all human beings have equal claim on each nation's care, protection, and money.

And finally, *New York Times* columnist David Brooks wrote a column about the Globalist-Nationalist debate titled "We Take Care of Our Own."[4] He summarized my *American Interest* essay and then improved upon it by showing how America in particular can easily formulate a patriotism acceptable to both sides. He notes that

America, unlike most other countries, was founded as a universalist nation. It has long been a source of pride that America takes people from many countries and unites them behind American ideals. Like Stenner, Brooks criticizes "the forces of multiculturalism" for damaging America's longstanding commitment to cultural union and assimilation. This damage left an opening, he says, for Donald Trump's unwelcoming nationalism, which has more in common with the kind of "European blood and soil" nationalism that is often overtly racist.

Brooks concludes that:

> *The way out of this debate is not to go nationalist or globalist. It's to return to American nationalism—espoused by people like Walt Whitman—which combines an inclusive definition of who is Our Own with a fervent commitment to assimilate and Take Care of them.*

Brooks' essay was published on July 15, 2016, six days before Donald Trump gave his acceptance speech at the Republican National Convention in which he painted a dark vision of America going to hell in a dangerous world. Trump's nationalism was all about "us" versus "them" and how we can kick them out or otherwise defeat them. It was the opposite of Brooks' recommendation; it was what Summers would call "irresponsible nationalism."

The Democrats, in contrast, in their convention, did exactly what Brooks urged. It is to be expected that the Democrats would feature speakers from all races, each waving the American flag symbolically or literally; that's normal convention showmanship. But for many viewers, the emotional highlight of the week occurred on Thursday, July 28, 2016, just before Hillary Clinton was introduced by her daughter, Chelsea. The speaker before Chelsea was Khizr Khan, an immigrant from Pakistan whose son Humayun joined the U.S. Army and fought in Iraq. Humayun died a hero's death, having stepped forward to intercept an approaching car loaded with explosives. He saved the soldiers under his command and possibly many more on the base they were guarding. His father addressed the convention and the country:

> Tonight we are honored to stand here as parents of Captain Humayun Khan and as patriotic American Muslims—with undivided loyalty to our country. Like many immigrants, we came to this country empty-handed. We believed in American democracy; that with hard work and goodness of this country, we could share in and contribute to its blessings.

Then, directly addressing his remarks to Donald Trump, who had said he would try to restrict Muslim immigration to America:

> Let me ask you [Mr. Trump]: have you even read the United States constitution? I will gladly lend you my copy. [He pulls out his copy from his jacket pocket.] In this document, look for the words "liberty" and "equal protection of law." Have you ever been to Arlington Cemetery? Go look at the graves of brave patriots who died defending the United States of America. You will see all faiths, genders, and ethnicities. You have sacrificed nothing and no one.[5]

Khan's embrace of America, its values, and its constitution was a stirring example of a kind of patriotism that can unite most nationalists and most globalists. It celebrates "us" without denigrating "them." It is welcoming and assimilationist. This approach may not work in countries that define themselves by the history of a single ethnic group. But with some tinkering it should work in Britain (which can take credit for having pioneered so many liberal institutions), in France (whose revolution was one of ideas and rights), and in other countries that have long traditions of openness, or of taking in refugees.

Diversity is difficult and often divisive. It's not shades of skin color that divide; it is the perception that people in other groups have different values, and that they behave in ways that violate our moral worldview. Among the most important divisions within many

Western nations is now the division between globalists and nationalists. The two sides have many real differences that must be worked out by a long and difficult political process. But political disagreements may become more tractable if both sides can understand each other a little better, and if both sides share a love of their country that is both passionate and—to varying degrees, perhaps—welcoming.

Notes

[1]. G. Monbiot, "The New Chauvinism," The Guardian, August 9, 2005, http://www.monbiot.com/2005/08/09/the-new-chauvinism/.

[2]. L. Summers, "Voters Deserve Responsible Nationalism, Not Reflex Globalism," Financial Times, July 10, 2016, http://www.ft.com/cms/s/2/15598db8-4456-11e6-9b66-0712b3873ae1.html#axzz4G1Sk80uZ.

[3]. D. Miller, Strangers in Our Midst: The Political Philosophy of Immigration (Cambridge, MA: Harvard University Press, 2016).

[4]. D. Brooks, "We Take Care of Our Own," New York Times, July 15, 2016, http://www.nytimes.com/2016/07/15/opinion/we-take-care-of-our-own.html.

[5]. http://abcnews.go.com/Politics/full-text-khizr-khans-speech-2016-democratic-national/story?id=41043609.

EVALUATING THE AUTHOR'S ARGUMENTS:

Based on the different viewpoints Jonathan Haidt mentioned and discussed in his concluding paragraphs, what do you think he believes is the best way to approach the globalist-nationalist debate? Reread the arguments made by George Monbiot, David Miller, and David Brooks. Which argument do you believe the author most agrees with? Why do you think this?

What Is Chauvinism?

Dave Wilton

"Chauvinism is an eponym, or a word formed from a person's name, in this case a certain Nicholas Chauvin."

As this viewpoint indicates, chauvinism is a term that has departed from its original meaning. Somewhere along the line, the term started to refer to sexism as opposed to superpatriotism. Dave Wilton offers an anecdote on a woman who wore man's clothes and went to a bar to protest for equal rights for all sexes. It gained greater popularity in the 1960s and 1970s when the feminist movement reached another peak. The term "chauvinism" is the eponym of a possibly fictional person named Nicholas Chauvin. It refers to extreme patriotism and has a negative connotation. The term originated after the exile of Napoleon Bonaparte, at which time Chauvin was believed to be a soldier who still wanted to blindly follow and revive the Bonaparte era. Dave Wilton teaches writing at Texas A&M University.

AS YOU READ, CONSIDER THE FOLLOWING QUESTIONS:

1. When and where was Nicholas Chauvin born?
2. What year did the word "chauvinism" begin to be used in English?
3. Who described the belief that our species is superior as "human chauvinism?"

Today we associate *chauvinism* with sexism, the belief that men are superior to women, but this is a relatively recent development in the word's history. The original sense of the word was superpatriotism, the blind, bellicose, and unswerving belief that one's country is always in the right.

Chauvinism is an eponym, or a word formed from a person's name, in this case a certain Nicholas Chauvin. No hard facts are known about Chauvin, and it is likely that he is a fictional character created to lampoon jingoistic patriots. The tales have it that he was born in 1780 in Rochefort, France and served ably and well in Napoleon's army, even being decorated and granted a pension by the emperor himself. After the Napoleon's exile to St. Helena in 1815, the name *Chauvin* began to be applied to those soldiers who idolized the former emperor and expressed a desire to return to the good old days of the empire. Most famously, the name was given to a ridiculous character in the Cogniard brothers' 1831 play *La Cocarde Tricolore* (The Tricolor Cockade), who uttered the line, "je suis français, je suis Chauvin" ("I am French, I am Chauvin").

Chauvinism and *chauvinist* crossed the channel and began to be used in English around 1870. As with the original French *chauvinisme*, the original English meaning was also extreme patriotism, first used in reference to France, as in the first recorded appearance in the *Pall Mall Gazette* of 17 September 1870:

> *What the French may have contributed to the progress of culture within the last twenty years is nothing in comparison to the dangers caused within the same space of time by Chauvinism.*

But quickly the term began to be applied to superpatriots from other countries, not just France.

The association with sexism was in place by the 1930s. The *Christian Science Monitor* of 7 August 1935 has:

> *Another correspondent objected to the same comment [...] She inquired pointedly if in reviewing "America's Young Women" we had suggested that it smacked of male chauvinism.*

After the French Revolution of 1789–1799, Napoleon Bonaparte (pictured at center) *became emperor of the French Empire. As emperor, he led the Napoleonic Wars of 1793–1815 to spread French revolutionary ideals to neighboring countries and gain more power for France.*

But *male chauvinist* may be a decade or more older, just unrecorded. There is this story from the *New Yorker* of 13 April 1940, but referring to an event that allegedly occurred some fifteen years earlier:

> *One night in the winter of 1924 a feminist from Greenwich Village put on trousers, a man's topcoat, and a cap, stuck a cigar into her mouth, and entered McSorley's. She bought an ale, drank it, removed her cap, and shook her long hair down on her shoulders. Then she called Bill a male chauvinist, yelled something about the equality of the sexes, and ran out.*

While there are these older uses, *male chauvinism* came to the fore with second-wave feminism of the 1960s and 70s, often with the added epithet of *pig*. For example, *Playboy* magazine ran this article heading in May 1970: Up Against the Wall Male Chauvinist Pig!

This association with sexism became so strong that often the *male* is simply dropped.

But *chauvinism* is not exclusively applied to sexists. It is also used in other contexts. In April 1955 the *Bulletin of the Atomic Scientists* decried the attitudes of those who professed a belief that their nation was superior to others in the field of science:

Even though scientists did not go as far as to confuse scientific knowledge with national ideological doctrine, they did, nonetheless, often make it a point of patriotic honor to practice a certain kind of scientific nationalism and almost indeed a scientific chauvinism.

Astronomer Carl Sagan in 1973 described the belief that our species is superior as *human chauvinism*:

Contact with another intelligent species on a planet of some other star[...] may help us to cast off our [...] human chauvinism.

A pretty successful eponym, considering it's named after someone who never lived.

Patriotism in the Face of War

Patricia Pulham

> "Patriotism is influenced by 'group emotion,' a feeling which...is at its most dangerous when it manifests itself in a rigid definition of what being patriotic means."

Violet Paget was a prolific writer and a fervent advocate of peace during World War I. She wrote essays for the *Nation,* the *Atlantic Monthly*, and other publications under the pen name Vernon Lee. She primarily focused on producing anti-war materials and on promoting empathy and mutual tolerance among countries. She eventually joined the Union for Democratic Control and published *The Ballet of the Nations* in 1915, an allegory and satire on World War I. In this viewpoint, Patricia Pulham highlights the menace that patriotism poses to peace as people isolate themselves from others and embrace violence to resolve conflicts. Patricia Pulham is a professor of Victorian literature at the University of Surrey in the United Kingdom.

AS YOU READ, CONSIDER THE FOLLOWING QUESTIONS:

1. How many British and German citizens died during the Battle of Arras?
2. Who was Vernon Lee?
3. What was the inspiration behind *The Ballet of the Nations*?

"Culture: A timely warning on the dangers of patriotism from the First World War," by Patricia Pulham, The Conversation, May 19, 2017. https://theconversation.com/a-lesson-on-the-dangers-of-patriotism-from-a-pacifist-of-world-war-i-76544. Licensed Under CC BY-ND 4.0 International.

When the Battle of Arras came to an end 100 years ago on May 16 1917, there was little for British and Commonwealth troops to celebrate. Though they had gained some ground in the trench warfare, the result was largely a stalemate, and there were an estimated 160,000 British and 125,000 German casualties.

Soon after, a translation of the Ballet of the Nations was published in a French pacifist journal, Les Tablettes. This morality play in which the dancers are the nations at war with each other, all driven by the ballet-master, Death, was written by Violet Paget under the pseudonym Vernon Lee.

A prolific writer who produced over 40 books in a career that lasted over 50 years, Lee has receded from public view. But her views on patriotism and pacifism are very relevant today.

Described by the writer George Bernard Shaw as one of "the old guard of Victorian cosmopolitan intellectualism," Lee was a polymath, adept at several languages, whose work encompassed aesthetics, art history, musicology, literary theory, travel writing, feminism, and politics, as well as the supernatural fiction for which she is perhaps best known.

Born to British parents at Boulogne-sur-Mer in 1856 she spent much of her early life in France, Germany, and Switzerland, before the family finally settled in Florence in 1873. On her extended annual visits to Britain, she moved in social circles that included such luminaries as Robert Browning, Oscar Wilde, Henry James, and William Morris, and she was well acquainted with Virginia Woolf and the young H G Wells. In the summer of 1914, Lee was on one of these visits when hostilities broke out, and found herself stranded in Britain for the duration of the war.

Warnings Sounded

In the lead-up to World War I, Lee had penned articles questioning the journalistic jingoism that inflamed nationalist fervour. When war broke out, perturbed by the escalating violence, she became an active member of a newly-formed pacifist group, the Union for Democratic Control. She continued to publish anti-war articles in leading journals such as The Nation, The New Statesman, the Labour Leader, and The Atlantic Monthly. However, her pacifism was soon to lose

Violet Paget (1856–1935) was a British writer who wrote under the pseudonym Vernon Lee. She expressed strong pacifist views in her writing during World War I.

her friends in Britain and abroad, as well as the professional support of publishers and editors.

Credited with introducing the term "empathy" into the English language, Lee often argued for the importance of mutual tolerance and respect among nations. On January 1 1915, four months after the Daily Mail proclaimed that German and Austrian music would no longer be played at British promenade concerts, Lee wrote an article for Jus Suffragii, the official journal of the International Women's Suffrage Alliance.

In it, she recounted how hearing Bach's music in a London church at Christmas had made her intensely aware of those many Germans in churches across "Bach's own country" who would have understood her thoughts and feelings. She argued that this shared cultural appreciation accentuated the affinity between the German and English peoples at the very moment "when war's cruelties and recriminations, war's monstrous iron curtain" had cut them off so completely from one another.

By Christmas 1915, war had made its powerful presence felt and, in response, Lee published Ballet of the Nations, a visceral allegory, illustrated by the English artist, Maxwell Armfield, in which the virtues and vices associated with war are personified and satirised.

Some years later, Lee explained how the Ballet was inspired by British responses to the sinking of the Lusitania, torpedoed by a German U-Boat on May 7 1915, an event which intensified anti-German sentiment in Britain.

Problems of Patriotic 'Group-Think'

Two years after the war ended, Lee's Ballet, revised and embellished, was republished in Satan the Waster, her philosophical meditation on World War I. The new version challenged the patriotic sentiment that had dominated public discourse during the conflict. Her commentary questioned those who extolled the benefits of collective thinking and the denial of individual resistance in the face of war.

In this later edition, Lee emphasised that the coupling of "patriotism" with a sense of national unity was especially problematic. She noted how patriotic sentiment depends on segregation and antagonism, on "being in" or "not being in," as she put it. She added that patriotism is influenced by "group-emotion," a feeling which, while it may bring nations a sense of unity and permanence, is at its most dangerous when it manifests itself in a rigid definition of what being patriotic means.

As a cosmopolitan thinker, Lee believed in the value of European unity and in highlighting those cultural similarities and exchanges that enrich human experience. She would have considered herself a "citizen of everywhere." As a public intellectual, in the run-up to World War I she used that sense of citizenship to voice her resistance to the herd mentality that was leading Britain to the brink of conflict.

As often occurs when governments insist on national unity to push their own agendas, her voice was increasingly silenced: then as now, Britain had "had enough of experts."

Political upheavals in the UK have today sharpened our focus on the problematic nature of "group-emotion" that has pitched Brexiteers against Remainers, and underlined the ideological dangers of "patriotism" recast as insularity. Lee's writings have much to teach us.

EVALUATING THE AUTHOR'S ARGUMENTS:

In this viewpoint, Patricia Pulham discussed the life and work of writer Vernon Lee (pen name of Violet Paget). What message do you think the author hoped to convey by writing about Lee? Lee advocated for pacifism during her lifetime. Do you think her argument for peace and mutual respect in wartime has merit? Explain your answer.

Chapter 2

What Can Patriotism Do for a Country?

WWII propaganda posters used patriotism to encourage Americans to join the war effort.

I WANT YOU FOR U.S. ARMY

NEAREST RECRUITING STATION

Global Patriotism Can Help Create a Better Future

Marcel J. Harmon

"However, I should note that patriotism for one's own country doesn't automatically equate to hostility against other nations."

In this viewpoint, Marcel J. Harmon makes a plea for global patriotism by delineating all the benefits of patriotism while also showing how it can take a turn for the worse. Patriotism is important to the survival of a country for many reasons, among them being the need to collect tax from citizens. Securing citizens' financial support helps a nation compete internationally. Patriotism also helps unify the citizens of a country. Nonetheless, patriotism can lead to negative impacts, which Harmon suggests is demonstrated by some aspects of the Trump administration. In this case, patriotism was used to promote xenophobia, racism, sexism and homophobia. Marcel J. Harmon is an anthropologist who co-leads the research and development team at BranchPattern.

AS YOU READ, CONSIDER THE FOLLOWING QUESTIONS:
1. How does *Merriam-Webster* define patriotism?
2. What are some past events that were fueled by patriotism run amok?
3. What is global patriotism?

"Patriotism of a Different Kind," by Marcel J. Harmon, The Evolution Institute, July 4, 2018. Reprinted by permission.

Another Fourth of July is upon us – that's Independence Day for any non-U.S. citizens whose lives don't actually revolve around what's going on in the States. It's time for fireworks, grill-fests, parades, flag-waving, and all things *patriotic*. But what does that word really mean? Merriam-Webster defines patriotism as *having or showing great love and support for your country: having or showing patriotism*. And patriotism is defined simply as *the love that people feel for their country*. Nation-states certainly benefit from citizens who love and support their country. From paying taxes to fighting and dying for one's country, such behaviors help ensure a nation endures and is competitive on the global stage.

From a cultural evolutionary perspective, patriotism, when felt by most of the citizenry, helps ensure that between-group evolutionary forces dominate over within-group forces at the level of the nation-state.[10] Patriotism helps ensure that greater degrees of competition occur between nations as opposed to between subgroups within a nation, which weaken it in the global arena. It does this in part through increasing member uniformity, often with a sense of urgency, in pursuit of the nation's common interests. And uniformity among group members (typically achieved in part via social/cultural norms) enhances a group's cohesiveness, cooperation, and functional integration.

However, I should note that patriotism for one's own country doesn't automatically equate to hostility against other nations. In actuality, there exists a continuum that ranges on the one end from generally peaceful coexistence and overall cooperation among nations composed of patriotic individuals (i.e., the European Union) to on the other end armed conflict among nations also composed of patriotic individuals. Along that continuum are cooperative allies who still compete economically or even occasionally spy on one another, as well as generally antagonistic nations who come together to participate in more friendly competitions at the Olympics. In all cases, patriotism increases uniformity among the citizenry, working against within-group forces.

Specific social control mechanisms involved include norms that encourage patriotism, such as reciting the pledge of allegiance in school, playing the National Anthem at sporting events, and

A sense of patriotic duty and civic responsibility is often invoked to encourage citizens to pay their taxes.

participating in Fourth of July celebrations. The transition across the liminal boundary separating childhood from adulthood, marked by rites of passage tied to U.S. citizenship like registering for Selective Service or registering to vote, can also encourage patriotism. There are other social control mechanisms that take more of the "stick" approach to discouraging "unpatriotic" behavior through various laws and norms. These range from disapproving sideways glances received for not removing one's hat during the national anthem to being executed for treason.

If we adopt Elinor Ostrom's eight design features that are the hallmarks of groups able to successfully cooperate, the norms mentioned above help define who we are as citizens of a nation. They address the first design feature—*establish a strong group identity, including understanding and agreeing with the group's purpose.* Peer pressure, gossip, large-scale boycotts, resulting in legal actions, etc. address the fifth design feature—*graduated sanctions to correct misbehaviors, which begin with friendly reminders and escalate only as needed.*

But patriotism has a dark side as well. It can be a particularly powerful unifier when coupled with an "other" perceived to represent a dangerous threat by those in power. The forced removal of Native Americans from their lands, the Japanese internment camps of World War II, McCarthyism and the Red Scare, shaming protestors for exercising their right to kneel during the National Anthem, and Trump's cruel immigration policy, were all arguably fueled by patriotism run amok. They harm citizens and non-citizens in the name of the state which is typically portrayed as under threat.

While such actions may unify a portion of the nation, they also usually have a unifying effect on other subgroups opposed to such actions. Such subgroups view the nation's common interests differently and express their love and support of country through resistance in various forms. This is another form of patriotism, and it's where I find myself personally. The many actions of the Trump administration worthy of resistance are too numerous to comprehensively list here, but include such things as dismantling the EPA, withdrawing from the Paris climate accord, supporting a tax plan that will exacerbate the divide between the haves and have-nots, seemingly starting a trade war, targeting the Office of Government Ethics, targeting the free press, fueling hate against minorities, undermining international alliances, the travel ban, and of course the cruel separation of immigrant children from their parents. Trump has chosen a path of divisiveness to appeal to his base, calculating that this will be sufficient for him to remain in power and further bend the presidency to his own apparently authoritarian leanings. He is betting that the dominance of within-group forces will ultimately benefit himself and his own—country be damned.

Resistance is necessary but won't be enough. We must also engage the other side to help tear down the in-group/out-group barrier. While engaging Trump's most vocal supporters may have little impact, positive engagement could likely be had with the many Trump voters who remain relatively silent. And honestly, it's past time to more deliberately look at tearing down such barriers at the international level. We need to view ourselves as members of the same species occupying a single planet with other species we depend on in one form or another. Humans have been effectively cooperating with one another and competing against "the other" since we were hunter-gatherers. But the threats humans collectively now face, many fueled by climate change, require more effective global cooperation.

As David Sloan Wilson has previously indicated, it's not enough for nations to be uniform and functionally effective for their own short-term success and/or long-term survival. The actions taken by nations in this pursuit sometimes negatively impact our species at the global scale—nations may benefit at the expense of the species as a whole. Global cooperation requires a means of effectively upscaling to the global level Ostrom's eight design features or upscaling other attempts to harness the social control mechanisms that evolved in our hunter-gatherer villages. A species or even planetary focused form of *patriotism* could be an important part of that.

So, this Fourth of July, I'll be patriotically resisting in some form the Trump administration, its policies, and its focus on a divisive, within-group strategy to maintain power. At the same time, I'll be looking for opportunities to express a global form of patriotism.

Sharing this article on the Fourth is one way I'll be doing both, and hopefully starting some conversations in the process. I'm curious what others are doing on the Fourth to resist the Trump administration or display a form of global patriotism.

EVALUATING THE AUTHOR'S ARGUMENTS:

In this viewpoint, Marcel J. Harmon writes: "the actions taken by nations in this pursuit sometimes negatively impact our species at the global scale." Do you think the author effectively supported this claim in the viewpoint? Do you believe global patriotism is indeed the answer to all of the issues the author raises? Why or why not?

"*[Jose Rizal] decided that love of country should supplant all other considerations, even that of his family or his own, or even of the woman he loved.*"

What Role Does Patriotism Play in a Country's Struggle for Independence?

Ma. Cielito Reyno

When a country is colonized, the question always remains: to whom do you swear your loyalty? Do you pledge allegiance to the colonizers or to the native people? In this viewpoint, Ma. Cielito Reyno depicts the life of Jose Rizal (1861-1896), a very important figure in the struggle for independence in the Philippines. Rizal, who is often described as a prodigy, produced critical work like the poem "To the Philippine Youth" and the essay "Love of Country." In the latter work, his growing sense of nationalism and devotion to Filipinos were palpable. He left the country, but only with the determination to return and lend a hand in the fight for independence. Ma. Cielito Reyno is a writer who covers Filipino history.

"For Love of Country," by Ma. Cielito Reyno, Republic of the Phillipines, September 19, 2012.

AS YOU READ, CONSIDER THE FOLLOWING QUESTIONS:
1. Who was Jose Rizal?
2. When and where was "Love of Country" published?
3. How old was Jose Rizal when he published his essay "Love of Country?"

Jose Rizal is said to have first expressed his sense of nation, and of the Philippines as a nation separate from Spain, as a young student in Manila. Proof of this, it is said, can be found in two of his writings. In his poem *"To the Philippine Youth,"* which he wrote in 1879, when he was 18 years old (and which won a prize from the literary group), Rizal speaks of the Filipino youth as the "Fair hope of my Motherland," and of the *"Indian land"* whose "son" is offered *"a shining crown,"* by the "Spaniard… with wise and merciful hand." Still in this poem, Rizal considered Spain as a loving and concerned mother to her daughter Filipinas.

In his memoirs as a student, later published as Reminiscences, he spoke of the time spent in his sophomore year at the Ateneo as being essentially the same as his first year, except that this year, he felt within himself the stirrings of *"patriotic sentiments"* and of an *"exquisite sensibility."*[1] He might have been only referring to the sense that the Philippines, was a colony of Spain, and as such, the Philippines was a part of Spain. If this were the case, his patriotism was therefore directed toward Spain for being the Philippines' mother country. Seen in another light, these words may have evidenced Rizal's moment of epiphany, his own portent of a future time when he would awake to the tragedies that were the lot of his fellow indios, the rightful heirs of the Filipinas their motherland.

Some cite Rizal's verse-play *"Beside the Pasig"* (written in 1880, when was 19), as his allegory of the Filipinos' bondage under Spain[2]; however, the play's protagonists are a young boy named Leonido, who defends the Christians, and Satan, who speaks against Spain for bringing Christianity to the Philippines.

As fate had it, Rizal ultimately awoke to the real state of the Philippines under the hands, not of a loving Mother Spain, but of an exploitative despot represented by the colonial government

The Philippines won its independence from Spain on June 12, 1898.
Philippines Independence Day is celebrated on June 12 every year.

in Manila and the friars who held great influence over the government. His awakening may have come by way of his own experiences at the university, his family's experience at the hands of the religious group that owned their farmland; and perhaps, from the stories about the reformist movement and the sacrifice of the three priests, collectively known as Gomburza, of ten years before. This last most likely were from his older brother Paciano, who had been close to Fr. Jose Burgos, and had been an outspoken critic of abuses during his years in college at the Colegio de San Jose.

Rizal saw the many injustices suffered by his fellow Filipinos: they depended on the religious corporations or on big landowners, for land to till, or for their living; people were afraid of airing their grievances or of talking or protesting against the friars or the government, in short, there was no real freedom of the press or speech. Most Filipinos lacked the privilege of education, and its resultant benefits, or if they did have education, this was the obscurantist kind generally propagated by the colonialist policy, which not only kept Filipinos in the dark about their rights, but worse, had molded them into an abject, submissive people ignorant or worse, ashamed of their own proud heritage, a heritage that existed even before the arrival of the Spaniards. Finally, Rizal realized that the Philippines had not been consistently represented in the Spanish parliament. For Rizal, this was the root of the absence of justice in the country, or of their being deprived of basic rights.

His essay "Love of Country" which he wrote in June 1882 (but appeared in the newspaper Diariong Tagalog Manila in August)[3], when he was already in Spain, and he was 21 years old. In it he talks of "love of country" which "is never effaced once it has penetrated the heart, because it carries with it a divine stamp;" that it is "the most powerful force behind the most sublime actions" and for that reason, love of country "of all loves…is the greatest, the most heroic and the most disinterested."[4] He speaks of the Motherland for whom "some have sacrificed their youth, their pleasures…others their blood; all have died bequeathing to their Motherland…Liberty and glory."[5]

It can be inferred from his words that at this point Rizal's sense of nation was now fully-formed and complete, and perhaps not by happenstance, its expression coincides with his departure from his country. While there is still no outright and open criticism of the friars, or the colonial government, or even of Spain for he may have only been being careful, Rizal by this time had become a nationalist and had gone abroad for the cause of his country-men. This is confirmed by a line from a letter written to him by his friend Vicente Gella, in the same month he wrote "Love of Country," (June 1882):

> "If the absence of a son from the bosom of his esteemed family is sad, no less will be that of a friend who, being very dear to all of us …his friends and comrades, now is away from us seeking the welfare that we all desire. Had it not been for that, the separation would have been more painful for the distance that separates us. May God help you for the good that you do to your fellow countrymen."

Another letter written by his friend Jose M. Cecilio, dated August 28, 1882, also corroborates this:

> "I'm very glad that you will go to Madrid where you can do many things in favor of this country jointly with the other Filipinos…so long as they will not give us freedom of the press, abuses, arbitrariness, and injustices will prevail more than in other parts of the world."[6]

Ultimately, it does not matter when or even how Rizal's polit-icization came, or why he went abroad: to complete his medical studies there; or, to expand his opportunities for establishing him-self as a writer[7]; or to embark on a career as an activist-writer who would use his pen to secure long-needed reforms in the social and political fabric of his country. And because the space for agitating for changes in the country was getting smaller by the day, it was time for him to leave. Under his leadership, together with the other Filipino youth, the Reform—or Propaganda movement—as it became known, flourished and triumphed. It triumphed not in the sense that it attained its main goals of obtaining parliamentary representation for the Filipinos, and freedom of the press, for these did not come to pass, but in the after-effects of its campaign, despite its apparent failure: other youths followed in their footsteps and took the next step—to begin the campaign for separation and independence. This was carried out by Bonifacio and the Katipunan, which launched the Revolution that, in turn, led to the birth of the Filipino nation.

And so Rizal became a crusader for his country's freedom. He decided that love of country should supplant all other considerations, even that of his family or his own, or even of the woman he loved. From his correspondence with friends and family, he remained constant to his Muse and his cause: the Motherland and her freedom.

When he had completed his education, and his formation as a son deserving of the Motherland, Rizal felt it was time to return to her. Friends and family stopped him from returning, but he was determined to do so, for he believed that the true arena for the fight was his country itself, not some foreign land.

Notes

1 Reminiscences and Travels of Jose Rizal [Manila: National Historical Institute, 1977] p. 21. See also Austin Coates, Rizal Filipino Nationalist & Patriot [Manila: Solidaridad Publishing House,] p. 36; and Leon Ma. Guerrero, The First Filipino [National Historical Institute, 2006] p. 53.

2 Rizal's Poems [Manila: National Historical Institute, 2002] p. 115; Guerrero, p. 79

3 Rizal's Correspondence with Fellow Reformists [Manila: National Historical Institute, 1992] p. 2.

4 Rizal's Prose [Manila: Jose Rizal National Centennial Commission, 1962], p. 18

5 Ibid., p. 19.

6 Rizal's Correspondence, op.cit., p. 4

7 Guerrero, p. 101-102.

8 Rizal's Correspondence, pp. 629-630.

9 Ibid., p. 314.

EVALUATING THE AUTHOR'S ARGUMENTS:

Jose Rizal believed that love of country should be valued above everything. Does the author of this viewpoint seem to agree or disagree with this sentiment? Patriotism is described as having both a good and bad side. What kind of patriotism do you believe Rizal was promoting? Support your answer with examples from the viewpoint.

Patriotism Is Mandatory in Wartime

Lumen Learning

> *"One of the first victims of nearly every American war is the First Amendment."*

American civil liberties are often restricted during times of war. In World War I, Congress introduced the Espionage Act of 1917 and the Sedition Act of 1918, which limited the freedom of Americans to speak against the government and protest war efforts. Even refusing to serve in the army was considered unacceptable under those acts. Violating the acts could put a citizen in jail for up to twenty years. The acts were also enforced in the United States mail operations, as socialist magazines like the *Masses* were denied distribution. Lumen Learning is a website that offers students free and affordable course materials, and in this viewpoint, it gives students an overview of the start and end of these war ordinances.

AS YOU READ, CONSIDER THE FOLLOWING QUESTIONS:

1. What is the difference between the Espionage Act of 1917 and the Sedition Act of 1918?
2. As discussed in the "Passing of the Acts" section of the viewpoint, why did the United States pass these laws?
3. What did the American Protective League urge German Americans to do?

Congress used the Espionage and Sedition Acts to stamp out war opposition by curbing civil liberties.

One of the first victims of nearly every American war is the First Amendment, which guarantees civil liberties encompassing some of our most essential democratic freedoms. The Espionage Act of 1917 and the Sedition Act of 1918 temporarily trumped Americans' rights to religious freedom and to freely speak, publish, or petition the government.

Acts to Control Liberties

The Espionage Act made it a crime to pass information with the intent of harming the success of American armed forces. To shore up the Espionage Act, Congress followed with the Sedition Act, which expressly prohibited speaking, writing, or publishing anything against the federal government and the war effort of the United States or its allies. This wide characterization of crimes included activities such as inciting insubordination, exhibiting disloyalty or mutiny, refusing to serve in the armed forces, or interfering with military recruitment operations. Those convicted generally received prison sentences of 5 to 20 years. The acts applied only to times, "when the United States is in war," and following the cessation of hostilities in November 1919, the legislation was repealed on December 13, 1920.

Passing the Acts

Wartime violence on the part of vigilantes, whether individual citizens or mobs, persuaded some lawmakers that laws protecting public order were inadequate. In their view, the public was making its own attempts to punish unpopular speech due to the government's unwillingness or inability to do so. Enhancing federal authority under the Espionage Act, followed by the Sedition Act, was therefore necessary to prevent mobs from doing what the government could not.

President Wilson and Attorney General Thomas Watts Gregory viewed the legislation as a political compromise. They hoped to avoid hearings that would embarrass the administration for its failure to prosecute offensive speech, but also feared proposals that would move prosecutorial authority from the Justice Department to the

War Department, creating a form of civilian court-martial saddled with questionable constitutionality.

The acts met considerable opposition in the Senate, almost entirely from Republicans such as Henry Cabot Lodge and Hiram Johnson—the former of the two defending free speech and the latter assailing the administration for failing to use laws already in place. Republican former President Theodore Roosevelt voiced opposition as well.

Enforcing the Acts

Attorney General Thomas Gregory instructed Postmaster General Albert Burleson to censure and, if necessary, discontinue delivery of anti-American or pro-German mailings including letters, magazines, and newspapers. The Postal Service followed this directive through a nationwide network of censuring officials, such as the New York City postmaster, who refused to mail *The Masses*, a socialist monthly, citing the publication's "general tenor." For the most part, however, enforcement was left to the discretion of local U.S. attorneys and action varied widely.

Vigilantism and Repression

Police and judicial action, private vigilante groups, and public hysteria compromised the civil liberties of many Americans who disagreed with Wilson's war policies. Attorney General Gregory supported the work of the American Protective League (APL), which was one of the many patriotic associations that sprang up to support the war, and in coordination with the Federal Bureau of Investigation, identify antiwar organizations and those it deemed slackers, spies, or draft dodgers. The APL curbed dissent at home by compelling German-Americans to sign a pledge of allegiance, as well as by conducting extra governmental surveillance on pro-German activities and organizations such as unions. In a July 1917 speech, Max Eastman complained that the government's ongoing aggressive prosecutions of dissent meant, "You can't even collect your thoughts without getting arrested for unlawful assemblage."

Emma Goldman (1869–1940) was an anarchist political activist and writer. She was charged with conspiracy to "induce persons not to register" under the Espionage Act in 1917.

Prosecutions Under the Acts

Famed labor movement leader Eugene V. Debs—the Socialist Party presidential candidate in 1904, 1908, and 1912—was arrested in June 1918 for making a speech in Canton, Ohio, denouncing military conscription and urging listeners not to take part in the draft. Charged with 10 counts of sedition, Debs defended himself eloquently but was found guilty and sentenced on November 18, 1918—exactly one week after an armistice ended the fighting in Europe—to 10 years in prison and loss of his right to vote for life. Despite his own electoral disenfranchisement, he ran for president again in 1920 from prison before his sentence was commuted in 1921.

In *United States v. Motion Picture Film* (1917), a federal court upheld the government's seizure of a 1917 movie *The Spirit of '76* on the grounds that its depiction of cruelty by British soldiers during the American Revolution would undermine support for America's wartime ally. The film's writer and producer, Robert Goldstein, was prosecuted under the Espionage Act and received a 10-year prison sentence and $5,000 fine, which was commuted to three years upon appeal.

The End of the Acts

The U.S. Supreme Court upheld the Espionage and Sedition Acts in the 1919 case, *Abrams v. United States*, although Justice Oliver Wendell Holmes used his dissenting opinion to comment on what came to be known as, "the marketplace of ideas," a theory that suggests only minimal government regulation of speech and expression is necessary because ideas will succeed or fail on their own merit in the same way a discerning consumer marketplace will eventually eliminate bad products. Congress repealed the Sedition Act on December 13, 1920, although those convicted under the law continued to serve their prison terms. Subsequent Supreme Court decisions, such as *Brandenburg v. Ohio* in 1969, make it unlikely that similar legislation restricting civil liberties will be considered constitutional moving forward.

EVALUATING THE AUTHOR'S ARGUMENTS:

The author of the viewpoint writes about vigilantes, who were people who took the law into their own hands and punished people they deemed a threat to the American war efforts. Do you think the author would call those people patriotic? Do you agree with the claims the author made to explain why the laws discussed were enacted? Explain your answer.

How Americans Should View Patriotism in This Global Society

"American patriotism depends on a unique set of ideals and characteristics that originate from American culture and history."

Sharon L. Wisniewski

The international opinion on the United States is dwindling, and the Iraq War (2003-2011) did not help. Moreover, because of globalization, the reputation of the United States should be viewed as a threat to its survival. The war in Iraq put a lot of pressure on patriotism as many Americans struggled to see a victory in sight. Rebuilding patriotism in a global economy is an important task. Sharon L. Wisniewski writes in this excerpted viewpoint that the war made it difficult for many to maintain patriotic loyalty in the country. She paraphrases author Betty Jean Craige and her urge for Americans to focus on having allegiance to the laws as opposed to fellow beings. Sharon L. Wisniewski is a colonel in the United States Army.

"Patriotism in America: Is It Changing?" by Sharon L. Wisniewski, US Army War College, March 12, 2007. Reprinted by permission.

1. According to Betty Jean Craige, when it comes to military decisions, how do most Americans feel about their leaders?
2. What book did Betty Jean Craige write on American patriotism and globalization?
3. Why does Walter Berns see tolerance as a threat to patriotism?

[…]

Patriotism requires conditions that a nation must meet to be suitable to facilitate patriotic loyalty.[1] In the past the US has shown an ongoing desire to live up to the principles set forth in her Constitution and this has facilitated the enduring loyalty of her patriots. However, today we live in a difficult era. As Arthur M. Schlesinger, Jr. said, "it is certainly true that never in American history before has the United States been so unpopular in the world, so distrusted, disliked and even hated."[2] America is not living up to her promise and the American patriot is working harder than ever to maintain his loyalty because the nation's effort to get back on track is questionable and the ongoing situation in Iraq is perhaps the most pressing threat to American patriotism.

The situation in Iraq is contributing to the degradation of world opinion towards the US. Concerning war, Betty Jean Craige writes that the majority of Americans are likely to trust the leaders in the assumption that the leaders know how best to achieve military victory.[3] Iraq has yet to result in what the public perceives as a military victory. When the administration declared an end to the hostilities in Iraq it got another war that it had failed to anticipate. The sectarian violence that followed was not expected and not planned for. One author writes, it was a failure of leadership and only with a public acknowledgment… and long overdue conversation,… why this war… cannot be abandoned without serious consequences,[4] will the US be able to recover from the situation and potentially gain back the national trust it will need to continue in the struggle.

The international reputation of the US is not something to be taken lightly. The interdependence of the world is increasing brought

Many Americans demonstrate their patriotism during Fourth of July celebrations, but how patriotism manifests in everyday American life is constantly evolving.

home by globalization. Having a reputation of increasing distrust from the international community will significantly challenge our place in a world where nations are increasingly interdependent. In this environment the idea of making patriots is complicated. American patriotism is now subject to scrutiny more than ever and some may be drawn away from the idea entirely, as the bond uniting people moves away from their country and what it represents to a bond of common interests that now crosses international borders due to advances in technology that have resulted in globalization.

Betty Jean Craige discusses what she believes will lead to success in a global society in her book, *American Patriotism in a Global Society*. She says that it will depend on the degree to which a society subordinates its individual cultural or national interests to transcultural and transnational laws and institutions.[5] It will also demand allegiance to laws vice an allegiance to men because they engender profoundly different political values. Whereas allegiance to men produces relationships of opposition to groups perceived to be alien, allegiance to law allows for cooperation between the group and other groups in the world, even group's historically enemies. This creates harmonious interaction in a global society.[6] For Americans, currently the only dominant world power, this subordination is a new concept.

American patriotism depends on a unique set of ideals and characteristics that originate from American culture and history. Craige suggest that for Americans to survive in a global society they must subordinate this heritage and this will require a paradigm shift. If however, you consider again the basic principles from which American patriotism originates it should allow, when properly applied, for being a good neighbor,[7] which is a mandatory trait for successful participation in a global society.

Additional challenges come from the idea of tolerance and multiculturalism. Since the 1980's schools have adopted teaching a multi-ethnic and polyglot concepts which is more in line with an increasingly interrelated world.[8] Children are educated in multiculturalism and tolerance which under cuts love of country.[9] Walter Berns sees tolerance as a threat to patriotism in that it discourages the patriot from loving those traits he feels are admirable about his own country because tolerance implies that no country is better than another. Multiculturalism is a threat to patriotism in that

FAST FACT

In 2018, a Pew Research Center poll found that American opinions are still split over the Iraq war fifteen years later, with 48 percent of Americans believing that the war was a bad decision and 43 percent asserting that it was the right decision.

it emphasizes maintaining ones cultural identity over any national loyalty. It gives higher priority to cultural and ideological pluralism than to a national unity. Multiculturalism supports cultures maintaining their identity in a larger society that desires to consume them. [10] It resists integration which seeks to produce a cultural amalgamation (national unity), which requires the submergence of a supposed original ethnic identity in a new, evolving culture.[11] As these cultural groups develop their ties extend beyond the boundaries of America and reach to those who share like cultural identities. The threat is that this will potentially diminish their desire or need to be part of the greater American identity. It is essentially a "systematic dismantling of America's unitary national identity."[12] It is a country's national identity that produces 'love of country" and forms the basis for patriotism.

These challenges are no less daunting than the challenges the patriot has faced in the past.

[…]

Notes

1 Igor Primoratz, ed., *Patriotism* (Amherst, New York: Humanity Books, 2002),102.

2 Arthur M. Schlesinger Jr., *Books: War and the American Presidency*, website, Washingtonpost.com; Internet; accessed 31 December 2006.

3 Betty Jean Craige, *American Patriotism In a Global Society* (Albany, New York: State University of New York Press, 1996), 31.

4 Joe Klein, "The Danger of Yellow Ribbon Patriotism", *TIME, Web Exclusive* (23 August 2005) |www.time.com/time/columnist/klein/article/0,9565,1096435-2,00.html, accessed 1 Jan 07.

5 Craige., 42.

6 Ibid., 30.

7 Ibid., 120. Craige says that today's patriot will best serve the nation by motivating the nation to be a good neighbor in a community of nations.

8 Phil Scranton, ed., *Beyond September 11th, An Anthology of Dissent* (Archway Rd, London: Pluto Press, 2002), 176.

9 Mary Walsh, "What Happened to Patriotism?" *Human Events* (21 May 2001): [journal online]; available from http://www.findarticles.com; Internet; accessed 14 September 2006.

10 Betty Jean Craige, *American Patriotism In a Global Society* (Albany, New York: State University of New York Press, 1996), 63.

11 Ibid., 64.

12 Ibid.

EVALUATING THE AUTHOR'S ARGUMENTS:

Sharon L. Wisniewski writes that "children are educated in multiculturalism and tolerance which under cuts love of country." Did the author support this claim well? Give three examples of benefits she sees to revisiting what children are being taught. What could be the potential disadvantages to this?

Viewpoint

5

Impoverished Americans Still Believe in America

Francesco Duina

"*So, although America's least well-off have reasons not to love their country, they hold it dear to their hearts and in many ways idealize it.*"

Most Americans who live in poverty are still patriotic. Francesco Duina reports that 80 to 90 percent of poor Americans see the United States as among the best countries in the world. This attitude transcends race, ethnicity, political affiliation, religion, and gender. People living in poverty in other developed countries don't hold their countries in such high esteem. Even the 2008 recession did not affect the attitude of those in the working class. In this excerpted viewpoint, Duina tries to make sense of what patriotism means to impoverished Americans in the face of adversity. Francesco Duina is a professor and chair of sociology at Bates College in Maine.

AS YOU READ, CONSIDER THE FOLLOWING QUESTIONS:
1. What is the fifth most dangerous city in the United States, according to this viewpoint?
2. Are impoverished Americans better or worse off than their counterparts in other developed countries?
3. Who are the two candidates who used the economic state of impoverished Americans to campaign for the 2016 presidential election?

Eddie, a fifty-six-year-old African American, lives in Birmingham, Alabama. Once a spelling-bee champion in school and "smart kid" who used to draw and love music, he now aspires to work in food services but earns less than one thousand dollars a month working at informal and irregular jobs, taking life day by day, and hoping—as his grandparents taught him long ago to do—that "maybe tomorrow will be better." Though he served in the army for three years, he receives very few benefits from the government. He resides in the fifth most dangerous city in the United States, where the poverty rate is more than 30% and robberies, aggravated assaults, and arson attacks are commonplace.[2] He knows that incomes for the people in the middle and lower classes in the country have been stagnating and believes that "the top percentage seems to be making all the money." There are problems in the United States, for sure, and "no society is perfect . . . we have our dark shadows." Still, despite all the difficulties in his life, he is convinced about one thing: America "is an exceptional country." Indeed, as he puts it, America is "the last best hope for mankind on earth . . . the last best hope for countries on earth."

Eddie is like millions of Americans. Many are poor and face serious adversity, and much in their lives is a daily struggle. They have access to very limited social services and support—partly a reflection of the fact that the majority of their compatriots, including those with very little, believe in the fairness of existing class differences. The odds that their children will enjoy a better life in the future are low. They also work very long hours while the gap between themselves and the rest of society, already considerable, continues to

Following Hurricane Katrina in 2005, many impoverished New Orleans residents were left without homes and with subpar living conditions. Nonetheless, many poor Americans remain patriotic.

widen. On these and other dimensions their situation is lacking in both absolute and relative terms: by many measures, America's poor are worse off than their counterparts in other advanced countries. To have no money in America is tough in itself, and tougher than being poor in most other rich societies.

And, like Eddie, these millions of impoverished Americans are highly patriotic. Given their predicaments, it could be reasonable to expect them to feel some dissatisfaction, if not resentment, toward their country. With the American Dream eluding them and little in their lives suggesting that things will improve, the American poor—understood in this book as those belonging to the most economically disadvantaged class in society—could understandably be critical of the society in which they live. In some respects, they certainly are. Many believe that, in a practical sense, a lot needs fixing—a sense of disgruntlement that the likes of Donald Trump and Bernie Sanders tapped into during their 2016 presidential campaigns.

But their fundamental belief in the country remains unshaken and, indeed, by any measure stunningly strong: 80%–90% of America's poor (and even more, depending on how exactly we define the "poor" and measure their "patriotism") hold the United States in high esteem. They are proud of their nation, believe in the greatness and superiority of the United States, and would rather be citizens of America than of any other country in the world. In fact, their patriotism—defined in this book as the opinion that their country is fundamentally better than other countries—is extraordinary. They are more patriotic than the poor in almost all other advanced countries in the world, even though the latter are in many ways better off than they are. In the United States their patriotism exceeds in many instances the patriotism of working-class, middle-class, and upper-class Americans. So, although America's least well-off have reasons *not* to love their country, they hold it dear to their hearts and in many ways idealize it.

The sentiment is widespread—cutting across race, gender, political, and religious lines. Patriotism is high among impoverished white, black, and other nonwhite Americans. It is high among poor men and women, liberals and conservatives, religious believers and nonbelievers. While there are certainly variations across regions of the country (in the Middle

Atlantic region, for instance, it is less widespread), their patriotism is high in absolute terms in every region of the country. It is also a resilient sort of patriotism: among all classes in the United States, the patriotism of Americans living in poverty has been affected the least by the economic crisis of 2008–2009, and by some measures it has actually increased.

This book is about Americans like Eddie and their patriotic views. It is about impoverished Americans and their intense love of their country. Why are America's poor so patriotic? Specifically, what attributes do they ascribe to the United States? How do they think those attributes shape their lives? What are the limitations that they see in other countries that make the United States superior to those countries? And, crucially, how do these Americans reconcile—if they in fact do—their own difficult situation with their positive view of the country? This is a book about what sociologists would call the "narratives" of patriotism among the poor: the conceptual threads, images, stories, and visions that the economically worst-off Americans articulate about their country. It is about their stories and perspectives. It is an effort to investigate, hear, and understand firsthand the logic and reasoning of this particular segment of the American population—a segment that our wealthy and extremely powerful society seems to have forgotten in many ways or to have left behind with little consideration.

[…]

EVALUATING THE AUTHOR'S ARGUMENTS:

In this viewpoint, the author asks: "Why are America's poor so patriotic?" How would Duina answer this question? What arguments would he use to support his claim? Why do you think impoverished Americans' attitudes toward their country vary from the attitudes of their counterparts in other countries? Support your claim with evidence from the viewpoint.

Chapter 3

How Does Patriotism Relate to Current Issues?

White supremacy and nationalism can be confused with patriotism, which has led to conflicts in the United States and other contries.

Viewpoint

1

Millennials and Patriotism

Gabrielle Bosché

"The Millennial generation has earned plenty of labels. Patriotic certainly isn't one of them."

Though each generation of youth has rebelled against conformity at some point, the grievances against millennials are different and won't change anytime soon. Millennials do not use the word "patriotic" to describe themselves. They do not wish to serve in the military. They view themselves more as citizens of the world than as patriotic Americans, and they do not believe the United States is the greatest country in the world. As explained in this viewpoint, Gabrielle Bosché believes the attitude of millennials is what makes this generation stronger than previous generations. Because of this attitude, they can help enact change in the country and can do more for society than previous generations. Gabrielle Bosché, who describes herself as a millennial, is the founder and president of the Millennial Solution, a strategy firm that helps companies attract, retain, and engage millennials.

"Why Millennials Aren't Patriotic," by Gabrielle Bosche, The Stream, July 3, 2017. Reprinted by permission.

1. What percentage of millennials shows no interest in joining the military, according to the viewpoint?
2. What are the three reasons the author gives to explain why millennials don't see themselves as patriotic?
3. How do millennials compare to other generations when it comes to describing themselves as patriotic?

I f you've ever wondered what's wrong with Millennials, it could be what they think about America.

Or maybe I should say it's what *we* think.

I am a Millennial living in our nation's capital. Washington, D.C. is looking her absolute finest this time of year. Bright red, white and blue blows throughout the streets and there is an air of excitement as locals and tourists pack together on the mall to watch the fireworks explode over the monuments.

The 4th of July is my absolute favorite holiday—but it isn't for many of my fellow Millennials.

The Millennial generation has earned plenty of labels. Patriotic certainly isn't one of them.

Every generation of youth rebels against the establishment. They push boundaries and question the decisions of those in charge. We say they're still "coming of age" or joke that "they haven't paid taxes yet."

But the lack of patriotic youth is different with Millennials, and it may not change anytime soon.

Millennials Don't See Themselves as Patriotic

Millennials aren't joining the military. A recent study found 85% of Millennials showing no interest serving in the military. Compared to Millennials, men from Generation X are twice as likely to have served in the military at some point in their lives. Baby Boomers are six times as likely. A young man who was born in 1963 was 11 times likelier to have served than a Millennial man is today.

Millennials don't consider themselves patriotic. According to Pew Research, only about half of Millennials say the phrase "a patriotic

Millennials are defined as individuals who were born between the early 1980s and the early 2000s. Their attitudes toward patriotism demonstrate a shift in what the concept means to Americans.

person" describes them very well—with 35% saying this is a "perfect" description. Just compare that to 64% of Gen Xers, 75% of Boomers and 81% of Silents who say this describes them very well.

In my 11 years of researching Millennials, I have discovered some interesting, inspiring and daunting truths about my generation.

Millennials are more likely to consider themselves citizens of the world than citizens of the United States.

Millennials do not believe in American exceptionalism… or at least they would be very hesitant to call America, "The best country in the world."

Millennials take a globalist approach to world affairs and are more concerned with how our actions are perceived and affected around the world than our parents were at their age.

The cause is threefold.

Millennials are less likely than other generations to associate with political parties, churches or affinity groups. We want to be seen as independent in our thoughts and actions and do not need to be associated with a particular country to feel like we belong here.

Millennials have been raised with anti-bullying campaigns and societal discussions about privilege and access. This has heightened our awareness to those who have and those who have not. This, mixed with how our history was framed in public and higher education has caused many in my generation to express disappointment in who we are as a world power.

And of course, we were given trophies for participating, which taught us that being #1 isn't the only goal of a game. It matters how you win the game.

Not All Is Lost

Not all Millennials have lost respect for our country. I know many young people (myself included) consider pledging allegiance to the flag a privilege, not a duty. This is not an editorial on what is wrong with my generation. In truth, I believe Millennials are more equipped to change the world than our predecessors were at our age. I believe our social awareness can be used for America's benefit, and our love of justice and pride for our country are not mutually exclusive.

As you celebrate America's birthday with your family and friends, consider what Millennials love about America may not be what you love about America. It's up to you to find out why.

EVALUATING THE AUTHOR'S ARGUMENTS:

Though the author identifies as a millennial, does she seem to identify with the way millennials feel about patriotism described in the viewpoint? By writing this viewpoint, is the author making a call to action? If yes, what is she urging readers to do? What statements might push a reader to rethink how he or she views patriotism?

What Does Patriotism Mean in the US Today?

Adam McCann

"Expressions of American patriotism come in many forms — from setting off fireworks during Fourth of July and buying American-made goods to paying taxes and serving in the armed forces."

According to the personal finance website Wallethub, Virginia is the overall most patriotic state in the United States. To draw this conclusion, the researchers took many factors into consideration, including enlisted military residents, active voters, and AmeriCorps volunteers per capita. Virginia is followed by Alaska and Wyoming, with Massachusetts making the list as the least patriotic state in the United States according to their methodology. In addition, the study revealed that red states tend to be more patriotic than blue states. Two factors were considered to complete this research: military engagement and civic engagement. The red state citizens were more likely to be engaged in those ways than citizens in blue states. Adam McCann, who reports on these findings, is a financial writer at Wallethub.

"2018's Most Patriotic States in America," by Adam McCann, Wallethub, Evolution Finance, Inc., June 26, 2018. Reprinted by permission.

AS YOU READ, CONSIDER THE FOLLOWING QUESTIONS:
1. What state has the most veterans per capita?
2. What state has the lowest percentage of adults who voted in the 2016 presidential election?
3. What state has the highest volunteer rate?

Expressions of American patriotism come in many forms—from setting off fireworks during Fourth of July and buying American-made goods to paying taxes and serving in the armed forces. But some states are better than others at showing their national pride.

So in order to determine where Americans bleed the most red, white and blue, WalletHub compared the states across 13 key indicators of patriotism. Our data set ranges from share of enlisted military population to share of adults who voted in the 2016 presidential election to AmeriCorps volunteers per capita. Read on for our findings, expert commentary and a full description of our methodology.

Most Patriotic States in America

Overall Rank	State	Total Score	'Military Engagement' Rank	'Civic Engagement' Rank
1	Virginia	70.48	5	10
2	Alaska	69.98	1	34
3	Wyoming	66.28	9	5
4	South Carolina	64.67	3	26
5	Idaho	62.99	8	11
6	Colorado	62.39	11	9
7	Hawaii	61.18	2	43
8	Washington	59.57	14	13
9	North Carolina	58.95	6	21
10	Georgia	58.76	4	41
11	Maine	58.02	28	3
12	South Dakota	56.57	21	16
13	New Hampshire	55.52	30	7
14	Oklahoma	55.28	7	31
15	Kansas	54.00	16	20

Overall Rank	State	Total Score	'Military Engagement' Rank	'Civic Engagement' Rank
16	Maryland	53.86	26	12
17	Nebraska	53.80	25	14
18	Arizona	52.84	13	29
19	Vermont	52.21	40	1
20	Mississippi	52.15	15	28
21	Utah	51.64	37	2
22	Nevada	51.45	19	27
23	Montana	50.70	17	32
24	New Mexico	50.30	20	30
25	Missouri	50.16	22	23
26	Alabama	50.10	10	44
27	North Dakota	50.09	33	15
28	Wisconsin	49.05	41	4
29	Iowa	48.05	39	8
30	Florida	47.87	18	40
31	Texas	47.81	12	47
32	Ohio	44.51	34	22
33	Minnesota	43.58	46	6
34	Arkansas	43.54	24	46
35	Louisiana	42.60	31	35
36	Tennessee	42.27	27	45
37	Kentucky	42.20	29	42
38	Oregon	41.94	32	37
39	Indiana	41.85	35	33
40	West Virginia	41.83	36	24
41	Delaware	41.24	23	48
42	Pennsylvania	39.81	45	17
43	Michigan	38.74	43	19
44	California	36.66	38	39
45	Connecticut	35.30	47	18
46	New York	29.82	50	25
47	Illinois	27.76	44	49
48	Rhode Island	27.24	42	50
49	New Jersey	26.70	49	36
50	Massachusetts	26.60	48	38

A traditional way for Americans to demonstrate their patriotism is by displaying the American flag on their home, office, or vehicle.

Highest Number of Military Enlistees

1. Georgia
2. South Carolina
3. Alaska
4. Idaho
5. Texas

Lowest Number of Military Enlistees

46. New Jersey
47. Vermont
48. Massachusetts
49. Rhode Island
50. North Dakota

Most Veterans per Capita

1. Alaska
2. Montana
3. Virginia
4. Maine
5. South Carolina

Fewest Veterans per Capita

46. Utah
47. Massachusetts
48. California
49. New Jersey
50. New York

Most Peace Corps Volunteers per Capita

1. Vermont
2. Montana
3. Oregon
4. Rhode Island
5. Washington

Fewest Peace Corps Volunteers per Capita

46. Alabama
47. Oklahoma
48. Arkansas
49. Louisiana
50. Mississippi

Highest Percentage of Adults Who Voted in 2016 Presidential Election

1. Maine
2. Wisconsin
3. Colorado
4. New Hampshire
5. Minnesota

Lowest Percentage of Adults Who Voted in 2016 Presidential Election

46. Texas
47. New Mexico
48. Tennessee
49. West Virginia
50. Hawaii

Highest Volunteer Rate

1. Utah
2. South Dakota
3. Minnesota
4. Wisconsin
5. Nebraska

Lowest Volunteer Rate

46. Louisiana
47. Nevada
48. New York
49. Mississippi
50. Florida

Blue States vs. Red States

Red states are more patriotic than Blue states.

- Red states: 23.57 average rank
- Blue states: 28.40 average rank

The smaller the number, the more patriotic a state is. States are designated Red or Blue based on how they voted in the 2016 presidential election.

Methodology

To determine the most patriotic states, WalletHub compared the 50 states across two key dimensions, including "Military Engagement" and "Civic Engagement."

We evaluated those dimensions using 13 relevant metrics, which are listed below with their corresponding weights. Each metric was graded on a 100-point scale, with a score of 100 representing the highest level of patriotism.

Finally, we determined each city's weighted average across all metrics to calculate its overall score and used the resulting scores to rank-order our sample.

Military Engagement – Total Points: 50

- Average Military Enlistees per 1,000 Civilian Adults Between 2011 & 2016 (No Prior Service): Triple Weight (~25.00 Points)
- Veterans per 1,000 Civilian Adults: Full Weight (~8.33 Points)
- Active-Duty Military Personnel per 100,000 Civilian Adults: Full Weight (~8.33 Points)
- Share of Civilian Adult Population in Military Reserves: Full Weight (~8.33 Points)

Civic Engagement – Total Points: 50

- Share of Adults Who Voted in 2016 Presidential Election: Double Weight (~10.26 Points)

- Share of Adults Who Voted in 2016 Primary Elections: Full Weight (~5.13 Points)
- Volunteer Rate: Full Weight (~5.13 Points)
- Volunteer Hours per Resident: Full Weight (~5.13 Points)
- AmeriCorps Volunteers per Capita: Full Weight (~5.13 Points)
- Peace Corps Volunteers per Capita: Half Weight (~2.56 Points)
- Trial- & Grand-Jury Participation per Civilian Adult Population: Full Weight (~5.13 Points)
- Frequency of Google Searches for American Flags: Quarter Weight (~1.28 Points) Note: This metric was adjusted for the total number of searches.
- Civics Education Requirement: Double Weight (~10.26 Points)

Sources

Data used to create this ranking were collected from the U.S. Census Bureau, Department of Veterans Affairs, Defense Manpower Data Center, Corporation for National & Community Service, Peace Corps, Military OneSource, United States Elections Project, Administrative Office of the United States Courts, and Center for Information and Research on Civic Learning & Engagement.

EVALUATING THE AUTHOR'S ARGUMENTS:

To determine the most patriotic states in the United States, the author points to two key variables: military engagement and civic engagement. Based on these variables, how would the author define patriotism? What traits make an American patriotic according to the author? Do you agree with this definition of patriotism? Why or why not?

What Republicans and Democrats Believe Patriotism Means

Kathy Frankovic

"Americans judge the level of patriotism in the country differently, depending on their partisanship."

In this viewpoint, Kathy Frankovic explores what it means to be patriotic. She explains that what patriotism means to Democrats differs from what patriotism means to Republicans. In addition, older generations feel like there is a decrease in patriotism in the younger generations. She notes that in reality the survey indicates that the number of Americans who define themselves as patriotic has not changed over the five years studied, but the number of people who would not call themselves patriotic has increased slightly. Moreover, the difference between the percentage of Republicans who describe themselves as patriotic compared to Democrats or independents has become more pronounced. Kathy Frankovic is a polling consultant who has worked with CBS News and other research organizations.

"Americans are patriotic – but differ on what that means," by Kathy Frankovic, YouGov, July 3, 2018. Reprinted by permission.

As you read, consider the following questions:
1. In what age group do Republicans outnumber Democrats?
2. What are some key points of difference between Democrats and Republicans in terms of how they view patriotism?
3. What are some factors that Democrats and Republicans agree on?

Seventy-six percent of Americans say they're at least somewhat patriotic. Americans like to feel patriotic. Four in ten in the latest Economist/YouGov Poll say they are "very patriotic." Three in four are at least "somewhat" patriotic. But what does being "patriotic" mean?

First of all, it makes a difference if you are a Republican. Republicans are more than twice as likely as Democrats or independents to call themselves very patriotic, and the gap is widening. Just under a third of Democrats and independents say they are "not very" or "not at all" patriotic.

Americans are nearly as likely as they were five years ago to call themselves patriotic. The number saying they are not very or not at all patriotic has risen only a bit since then.

Americans judge the level of patriotism in the country differently, depending on their partisanship. Republicans are almost twice as likely as Democrats to see the level of patriotism among all Americans dropping. Most Democrats say it hasn't changed lately.

For many, it's a cry for the country to go back to the way it was. The older one is, the more likely a person is to think the level of patriotism has dropped. Six in ten of those 65 and older say the country is becoming less patriotic. (Older Americans are also more likely than younger adults to call themselves Republicans, and are the only age group in which Republicans outnumber Democrats.) But half of those between 45 and 64 also think the level of patriotism in the country has declined.

But what does patriotism mean? There are many Americans who agree that one can criticize the government, and even disobey laws one disagrees with or think are immoral. But in nearly all cases, Democrats are more willing than Republicans to allow these actions.

Flag burning as a form of protest became prominent during the Vietnam War (1955–1975), but it has long been a controversial act among Americans.

There is only one thing on the list that more Republicans believe one can do and still be considered patriotic: criticize former Democratic President Barack Obama. Both Democrats and Republicans think criticism of President Obama is acceptable for patriots, but the GOP percentage saying this has increased nine points in the last year. Majorities of both Republicans and Democrats believe a person can criticize Donald Trump and still be patriotic, too, and those partisan percentages haven't changed much in the last year.

But if that criticism of American leaders is made outside the US, partisans disagree. A majority of Democrats say you can be patriotic if you criticize US leaders to foreigners, a majority of Republicans' disagree.

This marks a change for Republicans since 2013, when there was a Democratic President. Then, half of Republicans believed one could be patriotic and criticize the country's leaders abroad, and there was no difference in the opinions of Republicans and Democrats.

The gap in opinion between Republicans and Democrats is especially large when it comes to disobeying laws and refusing to serve in the military if one thinks the law or the war is unjust. But majorities in both parties reject a patriot refusing to pay taxes.

Flag burning, seen during protests against the Vietnam War, also shows a large party difference, though Democrats are still negative on whether a patriotic person can burn the flag. (Republicans and Democrats also have broad disagreements of football players "taking a knee" in protest during the playing of the National Anthem.)

Despite their political differences on what patriotism means—and whether or not they are patriotic themselves—Republicans and Democrats will be doing pretty much the same thing on the Fourth of July this year. It's a day to stay home and relax, to get together with family and friends and maybe have a cookout. A few more Republicans might attend a fireworks display, a few more Democrats go to a parade. But those differences are extremely small.

EVALUATING THE AUTHOR'S ARGUMENTS:

In this viewpoint, Frankovic claims "there is only one thing on the list that more Republicans believe one can do and still be considered patriotic: criticize former Democratic President Barack Obama." What might the author be implying with this statement? What other statements does she make that might reveal her opinion on this?

Marxism Is Not Un-American

Bhaskar Sunkara

In this viewpoint, Bhaskar Sunkara explains how capitalism has been considered an essential American characteristic for years. After World War II, efforts were made in the United States to prevent capitalism from smothering the working class. There was a healthy economic boost following the war, which made it appear that everyone could get a piece of the pie. This does not mean that the downfalls of capitalism, such as poverty and exploitation, did not exist. In fact, the promises that capitalism fostered failed to persist through the decades, and the 2008 recession revealed how fragile these promises were. Because of this, Marxist ideas and thoughts are gaining in popularity with people between the ages of eighteen and thirty in the US, challenging the conventional relationship between America and capitalism. Bhaskar Sunkara, the founding editor of *Jacobin* and a columnist at the *Guardian*, writes about the roles of Marxism and capitalism today.

> *"Marxism in America needs to be more than an intellectual tool for mainstream commentators befuddled by our changing world."*

"Why the ideas of Karl Marx are more relevant than ever in the 21st century," by Bhaskar Sunkara, Guardian News & Media Limited. Reprinted by permission.

Capital used to sell us visions of tomorrow. At the 1939 World's Fair in New York, corporations showcased new technologies: nylon, air conditioning, fluorescent lamps, the ever-impressive View-Master. But more than just products, an ideal of middle-class leisure and abundance was offered to those weary from economic depression and the prospect of European war.

The Futurama ride even took attendees through miniature versions of transformed landscapes, depicting new highways and development projects: the world of the future. It was a visceral attempt to renew faith in capitalism.

In the wake of the second world war, some of this vision became a reality. Capitalism thrived and, though uneven, progress was made by American workers. With pressure from below, the state was wielded by reformers, not smashed, and class compromise, not just class struggle, fostered economic growth and shared prosperity previously unimaginable.

Exploitation and oppression didn't go away, but the system seemed not only powerful and dynamic, but reconcilable with democratic ideals. The progress, however, was fleeting. Social democracy faced the structural crisis in the 1970s that Michal Kalecki, author of The Political Aspects of Full Employment, predicted decades earlier. High employment rates and welfare state protections didn't buy off workers, it encouraged militant wage demands. Capitalists kept up when times were good, but with stagflation—the intersection of poor growth and rising inflation—and the Opec embargo, a crisis of profitability ensued.

An emergent neoliberalism did curb inflation and restore profits, but only through a vicious offensive against the working class. There were pitched battles waged in defense of the welfare state, but our era has largely been one of deradicalization and political

Karl Marx (1818–1883) was a German philosopher, economist, and political theorist who established Marxist socioeconomic theory.

acquiescence. Since then, real wages have stagnated, debt soared, and the prospects for a new generation, still wedded to a vision of the old social-democratic compact, are bleak.

The 1990s technological boom brought about talk of a light and adaptive "new economy," something to replace the old Fordist workplace. But it was a far cry from the future promised at the 1939 World's Fair.

The 2008 recession shattered those dreams, anyway. Capital, free of threats from below, grew decadent, wild, and speculative.

For many in my generation, the ideological underpinnings of capitalism have been undermined. That a higher percentage of Americans between the ages of 18 and 30 have a more favorable opinion of socialism than capitalism at least signals that the cold war era conflation of socialism with Stalinism no longer holds sway.

At an intellectual level, the same is true. Marxists have gained a measure of mainstream exposure: Foreign Policy turned to Leo Panitch, not Larry Summers, to explain the recent economic crisis; and thinkers like David Harvey have enjoyed late career renaissances. The wider recognition of thought "left of liberalism"—of which the journal I edit, Jacobin, is a part—isn't just the result of the loss of faith in mainstream alternatives, but rather, the ability of radicals to ask deeper structural questions and place new developments in historical context.

Now, even celebrated liberal Paul Krugman has been invoking ideas long relegated to the margins of American life. When thinking about automation and the future of labor, he worries that "it has echoes of old-fashioned Marxism—which shouldn't be a reason to ignore facts, but too often is." But a resurgent left has more than worries, they have ideas: about the reduction of working time, the decommodification of labor, and the ways in which advances in production can make life better, not more miserable.

This is where what's evolving, however awkwardly, into the 21st-century socialist intellectualism shows its strengths: a willingness to present a vision for the future, something deeper than mere critique. But intellectual shifts don't mean much by themselves.

A survey of the political landscape in America, despite Occupy's emergence in 2011, is bleak. The labor movement has shown some signs of life, especially among public sector workers combating austerity, but these are at best rearguard, defensive struggles. Unionization rates continue to decline, and apathy, not revolutionary fervor, reigns.

Marxism in America needs to be more than an intellectual tool for mainstream commentators befuddled by our changing world. It needs to be a political tool to change that world. Spoken, not just written, for mass consumption, peddling a vision of leisure, abundance, and democracy even more real than what the capitalism's prophets offered in 1939. A socialist Disneyland: inspiration after the "end of history."

EVALUATING THE AUTHOR'S ARGUMENTS:

By writing this viewpoint on the dwindling state of capitalism and the rise of Marxist and socialist thought in the United States, what might Bhaskar Sunkara hope to accomplish? What examples does he use to support his claim? Do you agree or disagree with him? Support your answer with examples from the viewpoint.

Nationalism and Hate

Heidi Beirich

> *"Massive demographic changes have been foisted on the American people, and they are changes that none of us ever voted for and most of us don't like."*

White supremacy has reached its peak in the United States. This pattern is largely fueled by the prediction that by 2044, white people will no longer make up the largest racial or ethnic group in the US population. The Trump election brought promises of tougher legislation against immigration and a guarantee that the 2044 prediction could be avoided, but so far, white supremacists fail to see progress being made toward this goal. Besides race, hate groups also target religion, sexual orientation, and ethnicity. In this excerpted viewpoint, Heidi Beirich writes that the Trump administration has aided in fostering those groups with the rhetoric they use and by taking symbolic actions against immigrants and minorities. Heidi Beirich leads the Southern Poverty Law Center's Intelligence Project.

AS YOU READ, CONSIDER THE FOLLOWING QUESTIONS:
1. As of 2018, how many hate groups existed in the United States?
2. How many people died in 2018 from radical right attacks?
3. What did former Attorney General Jeff Sessions do to restrict immigration to the United States?

The Ku Klux Klan (KKK) is an American white supremacist hate group that was founded in 1865 and has existed in three different eras. The latest era of the KKK began in 1946 and continues today.

White supremacy flourishes amid fears of immigration and nation's shifting demographics.

Surging numbers of hate groups. Rising right-wing populism and antisemitism. Mounting acts of deadly domestic terrorism. Increasing hate crimes. Exploding street violence.

That was the landscape of the radical right in 2018.

In the U.S., white supremacist anger reached a fever pitch last year as hysteria over losing a white-majority nation to demographic change—and a presumed lack of political will to stop it—engulfed the movement. White supremacists getting pushed off mainstream web platforms, President Donald Trump's willingness to pass a tax cut for the rich but failure to build a wall and a turn to the left in the midterm elections drove deep-seated fears of an accelerating, state- and Silicon Valley-orchestrated "white genocide."

Even Trump's opportunistic November attacks on a caravan of migrants moving slowly north through Mexico were seen as all talk and no action by the white supremacist and anti-immigrant movements.

"Starting to feel swindled by @realDonaldTrump," influential antisemitic writer Kevin MacDonald tweeted on Nov. 15. "He will get slaughtered in 2020 unless he does something serious for his base on immigration." White nationalist Richard Spencer, who infamously led a crowd of fellow racists at a Washington, D.C., meeting in Nov. 2016 with a toast and raised stiff-armed chant of "Hail Trump," was more blunt. Spencer took to Twitter in November to proclaim, "The Trump moment is over, and it's time for us to move on."

These fears and frustrations, heightened by U.S. Census Bureau projections that white people will no longer be a majority by 2044, helped propel hate to a new high last year. The total number of hate groups rose to 1,020 in 2018, up about 7 percent from 2017. White nationalist groups alone surged by nearly 50 percent last year, grow- ing from 100 chapters in 2017 to 148 in 2018. But at the same time, Trump has energized black nationalist hate groups—typically antise- mitic and anti-LGBT organizations—with an increase to 264 from 233 in 2017. Overall, though, the great majority of hate groups are those that despise racial, ethnic or religious minorities and they, unlike black nationalist groups, have a firm foothold in the mainstream.

The previous all-time high number of hate groups the Southern Poverty Law Center (SPLC) counted was 1,018 in 2011, when rage against the first black president was roiling. Amid the era of Trump, hate groups have increased once again, rising 30 percent over the past four years. And last year marked the fourth year in a row that hate group numbers increased after a short period of decline. In the previous four-year period, the number of groups fell by 23 percent.

When Anger Turns into Action
White supremacists' angry energy metastasized in the two weeks leading up to the midterm elections, when three radical right terror- ist attacks and one failed attempt at a mail-bombing spree shook the

country, leaving 15 dead. The overall death toll tied to the radical right rose in 2018 as well, as white supremacists in Canada and the U.S. killed at least 40 people, up from 17 in 2017.

Among these killings was the Oct. 24 murder of two black people in a Kroger supermarket by a white man who first attempted to attack a Louisville-area black church, but couldn't get in. Then, on Oct. 27, an immigrant-hating antisemite killed 11 at the Tree of Life synagogue in Pittsburgh 10 days before the election. Radicalized online, Robert Bowers, who like Spencer had soured on Trump, imbibed a popular white supremacist conspiracy that Jews are bringing non-white immigrants and refugees into the U.S. to accelerate "white genocide." Bowers voiced these lies on the social media forum Gab, a refuge for deplatformed haters. Also in the run-up to the election, a thankfully incompetent Facebook-using mail bomber who wanted to go "back to the Hitler days," targeted Trump critics and set the country on edge.

The violence was so shocking that CNN's exit polls found that three-quarters of voters said it was an important factor in their vote.

The midterms tended to validate hate groups' fears for the future. Many extremist candidates lost, including prominent anti-immigrant and anti-LGBT candidates. Even more angering to hate groups were the dozens of women—who an increasingly misogynistic hate movement sees as allies to "white genocide"—elected to the new U.S. Congress, including two Muslims and a senator from Arizona who is openly bisexual. For white supremacists, these newly elected officials symbolize the country's changing demographics—the future that white supremacists loathe and fear.

There were, however, some bright spots for extremists. Republican Ron DeSantis, who has a history of consorting with anti-Muslim groups and making racist statements, is Florida's new governor. Republican Brian Kemp, Georgia's new governor, ran on a hostile anti-immigrant platform. And Rep. Steve King, R-Iowa, who has repeatedly regurgitated white supremacist ideas, was re-elected. But in all cases the margins were narrow, and some in the GOP seemed to have finally acknowledged that racism and bigotry might not be good campaign fodder. King, for example, was rebuked by Rep. Steve Stivers, R-Ohio, the National Republican Congressional Committee chair, for racist tweets and comments a week before the election. "We must stand up against white supremacy and hate in all forms, and I strongly condemn this behavior," Stivers tweeted.

Trump Still Mainstreaming Hate

The organized hate movement may be showing signs of disappointment with Donald Trump, but the president, aided and abetted by Fox News, continues to push his noxious anti-immigrant and anti-Muslim ideas into the public consciousness—fueling fears of a forthcoming white-minority country.

A couple of weeks after the midterms, Trump reignited his rant against the migrant caravan, raging on Twitter: "There are a lot of CRIMINALS in the Caravan." It was just the latest in the president's long history of denigrating people of color from other countries. Trump has repeatedly made racist comments about Latinos, starting with his first day of campaigning when he referred to Mexicans as "rapists." In January 2018 Trump reportedly referred to Haiti and other black-majority countries as "sh*tholes." Longtime prominent white supremacist David Duke called those comments the "PERFECT TRUTH" on his Twitter feed. And Trump's earlier attacks on the migrant caravan, which included calling Central American refugees from violence "gang members" and part of an "invasion" of the U.S. aided and abetted by the Democratic party, were straight out of the hate playbook.

In August, Trump tweeted in support of white South African farmers who extremists falsely argue are enduring a racist murder spree by black people, and he ordered a State Department inquiry into the matter. This propaganda is used by white supremacists as a "canary in the coal mine" scenario for white people. Three years ago, it was white supremacist Dylann Roof, wearing patches of apartheid governments, who cited the "white genocide" fantasy to justify his mass murder of African Americans in a Charleston church, and in October it was Robert Bowers using the same logic to justify his mass murder at a Pittsburgh synagogue.

The mainstreaming of harmful and poisonous ideas has spread to Trump's allies, particularly those at Fox News. Tucker Carlson was the source of Trump's South African tweet. He gave wildly incorrect information on the issue on his show the night before the president's tweet, and he also hosted an apartheid apologist on his nightly program in May to discuss the so-called war on white farmers in that country. Carlson has used his program to engage in tirades against diversity, transgender people and, especially, immigrants.

Like white supremacists, Carlson has tied these bogeymen directly to demographic change. In July, Carlson said, "Latin American countries are changing election outcomes here by forcing demographic change on this country." Then in November, he said, "It is never true that diversity is your strength." In another broadcast, he told his viewers, "this is more change than human beings are designed to digest."

Carlson's Fox News colleague Laura Ingraham echoed this theme. In August, she said, "The America we know and love doesn't exist anymore. … Massive demographic changes have been foisted on the American people, and they are changes that none of us ever voted for and most of us don't like." No wonder Carlson is beloved by white supremacists such as Spencer as well as Andrew Anglin, who runs the neo-Nazi website the Daily Stormer. In May, Anglin called Carlson's show "Tucker Carlson AKA Daily Stormer TV," and wrote, "wow, someone important is reading my articles."

Fox News is Trump's megaphone as well as the source of many of his ideas. And his on-air allies Carlson and Ingraham, whom Trump watches religiously, have audiences between 2.5 million and 3 million viewers.

Most Americans are now fully aware that Trump is emboldening white supremacists and helping to grow their ranks. An October poll by the Public Religion Research Institute shows a majority believe Trump has "encouraged white supremacist groups."

But he's done more than that. He has installed people with extremist views into his administration, and their views are affecting policy.

The Anti-Immigrant and Anti-Muslim Movements Wield Real Power

Trump showed now former Attorney General Jeff Sessions the door immediately after the midterm elections, but not before Sessions had left an indelible mark on administration policy. During his time in office, Sessions led the charge against immigrants, speeding up the immigration court system to make it harder for people to remain in the U.S., referring to himself cases that used to be resolved by the Board of Immigration Appeals, ordering the Department of Homeland Security (DHS) to refer all illegal border crossers to the Department of Justice for prosecution, and ending a policy that granted asylum to most victims of domestic abuse and gang violence in their home countries.

Sessions, like others still in the administration, has a close relationship with anti-immigrant hate groups, including the Federation for American Immigration Reform (FAIR). A number of FAIR's former staffers have gone into the administration. Former FAIR leader Julie Kirchner is now ombudsman for DHS Citizenship and Immigration Services. John Zadrozny, another ex-FAIR employee, is now with the State Department. Ian Smith, formerly employed with FAIR's legal arm, resigned his position in August at DHS, but only after leaked emails linked him to white nationalists Spencer and Jared Taylor.

Other appointees and staffers have ties to the anti-immigrant hate group Center for Immigration Studies (CIS) and the anti-Muslim hate group Center for Security Policy. During his confirmation hearing, current Secretary of State Mike Pompeo faced questions about his connections to anti-Muslim figures like Frank Gaffney and Brigitte Gabriel. Gabriel's hate group, ACT for America, lauded Pompeo's confirmation, stating he "understands the threats our country faces." The group had earlier awarded Pompeo its "National Security Eagle Award." Gabriel has claimed that ACT for America has been granted standing weekly meetings with the White House.

Particularly devastating are Trump's immigration policies, pushed by his senior adviser Stephen Miller and copied from FAIR and CIS. Miller, who was the main advocate of the Muslim ban and family separation policy, was close to Spencer when he was in college and has long-standing links to anti-Muslim leader David Horowitz, dating back to when Miller was in high school.

Whether it is unending ICE raids, abolishing temporary protected status, calling for the end of birthright citizenship, separating families, increasing the number of detentions or sending troops to the border, the administration's willingness to enact vicious anti-immigrant and anti-Muslim policies is a travesty of American values.

[...]

EVALUATING THE AUTHOR'S ARGUMENTS:

In this viewpoint, Heidi Beirich theorizes that President Trump helped nurture hate groups in the United States. How does she support this claim? Does the author seem to agree or disagree with the administration? She ends the viewpoint with a comment on American values. What does the author seem to consider essential American values?

Athletes at the Center of the Patriotism Debate

"I am not going to stand up to show pride in a flag for a country that oppresses black people and people of color."

Anna De Fina

Sports have always been a platform for protests. Prime examples are Tommie Smith and John Carlos during the Mexico City Olympics in 1968, the "hands up, don't shoot" pose by St. Louis Rams football players in 2014, and Colin Kaepernick's kneeling protests that started in 2016. Nevertheless, this last example amplified the intersection of sports and politics because it gained widespread national attention. Above all, Anna De Fina asserts, what makes these protests vital is that they rely on gestures as opposed to words. In this viewpoint, De Fina explains that the "patriotism" card has been used to rally the public against the players, since unpatriotic behavior is an offense many Americans find unforgivable. Anna De Fina is the chair of the Italian department at Georgetown University.

AS YOU READ, CONSIDER THE FOLLOWING QUESTIONS:
1. Who was Mike Brown?
2. Why has Colin Kaepernick's movement gained national attention?
3. What did Vice President Mike Pence do at a football game on October 7, 2017?

Recent protests by African American football players belonging to the American National Football League (NFL) have brought to light the significance of gesture as a form of political stance-taking and as an effective medium of communication. They have also emphasized that people's interpretations of what public gestures mean and the importance attributed to them are deeply influenced by wide social, political and historical contexts in which power relations play a central role. Silent gestures of protest are not a new phenomenon in sports, particularly when it comes to African American athletes and their status as citizens and members of American society.

A Small History of Gestures as Political Activism

Many in my generation will certainly remember an iconic and famous photo of Tommie Smith and John Carlos, two track athletes who won the gold and bronze medal in the Mexico City Olympics of 1968. In the picture the two men are shown standing on the podium, looking down with their fists raised during the playing of "*The Star-Spangled Banner*." Another famous photo, taken a few years later, in 1972, portrays another pair of track athletes, Vince Matthews and Wayne Collett, also African Americans, standing on the podium during the playing of the anthem in a relaxed posture that was defined in a Times editorial as "slouching" and "defiant."

Gestures of protest by athletes have multiplied since political activists in the United States have raised awareness of widespread police brutality against African Americans in the country, particularly after the shooting deaths of many young African American have been brought to light. Thus, for example, in 2014, members of the St.

Colin Kaepernick (pictured at center) *and other NFL players have kneeled in protest during the national anthem at NFL games since 2016.*

Louis Rams football team raised their arms in a "hands up, don't shoot" pose as they walked onto the field before a football game. On the same occasion, another player from the same team put white tape around his arms with the following words written on it "Mike Brown" and "My Kids Matter." The writings evoked the death of an African American youth shot by the police in the same year and the popular slogan "black lives matter," created in response to the killing of another young black man, Trevor Martin, after the acquittal of his shooter.

In recent times African American athletes have escalated their use of the strategy of symbolically drawing attention to social injustice through body language. In August 2016 Colin Kaepernick, then a quarterback for the San Francisco 49ers, took a defiant stance by sitting down while the national anthem was played before the start of games. He later said to the NFL media *"I am not going to stand up to show pride in a flag for a country that oppresses black people and people of color. To me, this is bigger than football and it would be selfish on my part to look the other way. There are bodies in the street and people getting paid leave and getting away with murder."* Kaepernick paid for his gesture by losing his job, but he inspired many other athletes to do the same and after his protest, many NFL players have continued to kneel when the National Anthem is played.

But while these actions in the past have been mostly discussed in the world of sports, recently they have been brought to national attention by Donald Trump through speeches and tweets. He started on September 22, when, addressing a crowd in Alabama, he asked his audience, *"Wouldn't you love to see one of these NFL owners, when somebody disrespects our flag, to say, 'Get that son of a bitch off the field right now. He is fired. He's fired!'"* He then continued his attacks with a series of twitter messages arguing that NFL team owners should compel players to stand up, that the African American players are *"disrespecting"* the *"beautiful"* American anthem, the flag and the country and that they should be thankful for making millions of dollars instead of protesting. As a response to those tweets, NFL players from many different teams chose a variety of gestures of protest starting on the Sunday following the Atlanta speech: from kneeling, to standing with interlaced arms to staying in the locker rooms during the playing of the National Anthem. A next chapter in the symbolic battle, was the widely publicized gesture by Mike Pence, vice-president of the US, who left the stadium during a football game on October 7 when players did not stand for the anthem.

The Battle Around the Protest

The battle around the protest of football players underscores the great significance that gestures of protest can acquire in specific historical moments and contexts and such prominence explains the violent reactions that dominant economic and political powers unleash against the actors who adopt them. Gestures are part of all cultures and often they turn out to be more effective than words because being inherently ambiguous they can be read in many ways. At the same time, gestures have historical significance because they evoke other gestures and remit to past struggles carried out by members of the same group to which the protesters belong. So when African Americans in the US raise their fists, we are reminded of the struggles of many other African Americans who performed the same gesture during the civil protests of the sixties and seventies, and thus they reaffirm a link between their condition today and their condition then. But because gestures are such an integral and natural part of human communication, they do not always receive the attention that those made by the NFL players protesters have received.

This points to the fact that it takes particular circumstances and stages to turn gestures into powerful tools of expression. The stage of national or international sports is one that can hardly be ignored because it is at the center of multimillion dollar businesses. Football teams in the US draw millions of fans and generate millions in revenue. As a consequence, everything that goes on in a football stadium has the potential for reaching huge audiences. In that sense, although racial inequality permeates all layers of American society, pointing to it in the world of sports turns out to be particularly dangerous for the status quo. It is dangerous because it draws attention to concrete manifestations of inequality. For example in the case of football, it may remind people of the fact that African Americans constitute the great majority among team members, but do not own one single team since all owners, with no exception, are white. It is dangerous because it demonstrates that racial solidarity can reach across the borders created by power and money leading individuals who are supposed to buy into a certain system to question it.

Finally, it is dangerous because it threatens existing hierarchies between players and those who "own" them. Thus, when Trump tells African American football players that they should be grateful for earning huge sums of money, he is basically telling them that they should shut up and play, forget who they are and accept the perverse mechanism that turns sports a money making businesses and them into instruments of that process. The fact that NFL players, the protagonist of the most American of sports, not only have not shut up but are receiving a great deal of media attention explains why Trump, who picks his enemies very carefully with ratings and audiences in mind, felt compelled to intervene and did so by playing an old but popular card: patriotism. In this version of patriotism, allegiance to the symbols of the nation (in this case the flag and the anthem) and to its supreme defender (the army) needs to be unconditional and without reserve. Thus, those who raise any doubts about the ability of the nation to represent them are automatically accused of being unpatriotic and often also of betraying those principles that animate the military, leading soldiers to supreme sacrifices in name of the community. Thus, patriotism is basically identified with critical acceptance of an abstract concept of nation and of its symbols. NFL players' protests point to a very different view: a perspective from which national unity is not a given but needs to be constructed and affirmed around principles such as justice and equality. This different conceptualization implies that citizens have the right and the duty to show their inconformity when principles that they regard as fundamental to democracy are broken.

Invoking Patriotism

The strategy of invoking patriotism is, however, a very powerful one in a country where nationalism is taught as a supreme value starting from infancy through school education and the repetition of rituals throughout key moments in individual and collective life, and continuously evoked through the ubiquitous display of the American flag not only on national buildings, but as often, in private homes and dwellings. Thus, lack of patriotism is something that many sports fans cannot forgive even in their most beloved champions. Playing this card has therefore been a very effective means through which Donald Trump and his followers have put pressure on team owners and players in order to terminate their insubordination. Together with these attacks centered on American "values," Trump has used direct threats of economic sanctions against the teams and of future boycotts on games, thus prompting the league's Commissioner Roger Goodell to try and negotiate a resolution to the conflict.

It is not clear whether these strategies will produce the intended result of silencing the dissenting voices. What is clear instead is that social and economic inequalities will not only continue to reign in the US but that they will be intensified under the Trump presidency. At the same time, a debate on the issues raised by the players has started to raise to national prominence drawing many to take position in favor of the African American NFL team members. Thus, no matter how things end, players protesting injustice have successfully broken the silence on the relationships between sports, race and inequality and without uttering a word but by using the power of their body they have managed to open a national conversation that should have started long time ago.

EVALUATING THE AUTHOR'S ARGUMENTS:

In this viewpoint, Anna De Fina covers the history of gestures by athletes as political protest. What claims does the author make in regard to the conditions of black lives in the United States? How does she support her claim? Based on the viewpoint, what does the author seem to believe about protests and patriotism? Do you agree with her? Explain your answer.

Facts About Patriotism

Editor's note: These facts can be used in reports to add credibility when making important points or claims.

A Brief History of Patriotism

Unlike other countries, the United States was founded on the notion that people from different creeds and nations could migrate here and pledge allegiance to this country.

According to *Encyclopedia Britannica*:

- Jean-Jacques Rousseau (1712–1778), who was a writer and philosopher, wrote many novels and treaties that inspired the French Revolution. He offered a new way to think of the world, which give light to patriotism and ended feudalism.
- Niccolò Machiavelli (1469–1527) also championed common liberty and the rights of common people to stand up for themselves.

Laws and Patriotism

The Bill of Rights includes the first amendments added to the American Constitution since its enactment in 1789. It consists of ten amendments securing the rights of every American, including the right to own a weapon.

According to Cornell Law School:

- The First Amendment states: Congress shall make no law respecting an establishment of religion, or prohibiting the free exercise thereof; or abridging the freedom of speech, or of the press; or the right of the people peaceably to assemble, and to petition the government for a redress of grievances.
- During World War I, the United States Congress passed the Espionage Act of 1917, which limited citizens' ability to interfere with the war efforts, including military recruitment.
- The following year, Congress passed the Sedition Act of 1918, which directly affected citizens' ability to speak freely of the war.

According to the US Department of Justice, after the September 11, 2001, terrorist attack, the United States enacted the USA Patriot Act, which allows the Federal Bureau of Investigation to adopt the same techniques used for organized crimes to investigate terrorism. This meant that the FBI could monitor activities of citizens they deemed suspicious of terrorist affiliation. The act also extended the punishment for terrorism-related crimes.

Debated Cases of Patriotism and Freedom of Expression
The Dixie Chicks

As reported by NPR, the Dixie Chicks is an American country music group formed by lead singer Natalie Maines and instrumentalists Emily Robison and Martie McGuire. In 2003, during a performance in London, Maines stated to the audience that she was ashamed to be from the same state as former President George W. Bush. The comment drew heavy criticism; country music radio stopped playing their songs, and fans boycotted their music and their concerts. The band was seen as unpatriotic. Moreover, public demonstrations against the Dixie Chicks included the burning of their CDs.

In 2006, Director Barbara Kopple released a documentary titled *Shut Up and Sing* about the incident that led to the backlash against the Dixie Chicks. In an interview with NPR, Kopple mentioned that the backlash was due to Americans' unwillingness, at the time, to oppose the Bush Administration on terrorism, since the 9/11 attack was still very recent.

Colin Kaepernick

According to Biography.com, in 2016, Colin Kaepernick—who was then the quarterback for San Francisco's 49ers football team—began a form of protest that involved kneeling during the singing of the national anthem before NFL games. The protest was to express his disapproval over the unarmed killings of black people by police officers. Other players ended up joining the protest, but most of the attention was on Kaepernick. This controversial act led to the end of his career following that NFL season. It is not the first time that sports and patriotism collided. Muhammad Ali drew controversy in the 1960s for refusing to fight in the Vietnam War.

Organizations to Contact

The editors have compiled the following list of organizations concerned with the issues debated in this book. The descriptions are derived from materials provided by the organizations. All have publications or information available for interested readers. The list was compiled on the date of publication of the present volume; the information provided here may change. Be aware that many organizations take several weeks or longer to respond to inquiries, so allow as much time as possible for the receipt of requested materials.

The American Legion
700 N. Pennsylvania Street
PO Box 1055
Indianapolis, IN 46206
phone: (317) 630-1298
website: www.legion.org
The American Legion is a governmental organization dedicated to veterans and to promoting patriotism in American communities.

Boys and Girls Clubs of America
1275 Peachtree Street NE
Atlanta, GA 30309-3506
phone: (404) 487-5700
website: www.bgca.org
The Boys and Girls Club of America is a safe haven for kids that teaches them how to be helpful members of their community.

Boy Scouts of America
1325 W. Walnut Hill Lane
Irving, TX 75038
phone: (972) 580-2000
email: MyScouting@scouting.org
website: www.scouting.org
The Boy Scouts of American (or BSA), which now accepts girls as

part of its programs, is a youth organization focused on helping kids from fifth grade to high school build ethical qualities that are deemed essential for good citizens.

Daughters of the American Revolution (DAR)
1776 D Street NW
Washington, DC 20006
phone: (202) 628-1776
website: www.dar.org
The Daughters of the American Revolution (DAR) is an organization that was founded in 1890. The goal of the organization is to preserve history and build patriotism. Women ages eighteen and up who can trace their lineage to a patriot of the American Revolution are welcome to join it.

Disabled American Veterans (DAV)
3725 Alexandria Pike
Cold Spring, KY 41076
phone: (877) 426-2838
website: www.dav.org
The Disabled American Veterans (DAV) is a nonprofit organization dedicated to helping American veterans and their family in any way possible.

Girl Scouts of the United States of America
420 Fifth Avenue
New York, New York, 10018
phone: (212) 852-5055
email: girlscoutcentral@girlscouts.org
website: www.girlscouts.org
Girl Scouts is an organization to help girls develop leadership skills and build community values.

For Further Reading

Books

Bryant, Howard. *The Heritage: Black Athletes, a Divided America, and the Politics of Patriotism*. Boston, MA: Beacon Press, 2018. Howard Bryant writes about how race, politics, and sports intersect in this book. Most importantly, he covers the slippery slope black athletes encounter when taking a stand.

Hansen, Jonathan. *The Lost Promise of Patriotism: Debating American Identity, 1890-1920*. Chicago, IL: University of Chicago Press, 2003. Jonathan Hansen uses the story of important American figures like W. E. B. Dubois, John Dewey, and Jane Addams to make the case for cosmopolitan patriotism.

Hanson, Victor Davis. *The Case for Trump*. New York, NY: Basic Books, 2019. The award-winning historian Victor Davis Hanson argues that Trump is a successful president. In this book, he explains the opportunity Trump saw in helping working-class Americans and in taking the unpopular stand necessary for the well being of the country.

Hayward, Steven F. *Patriotism Is Not Enough: Harry Jaffa, Walter Berns, and the Arguments that Redefined American Conservatism*. New York, NY: Encounter Books, 2017. Steven F. Hayward recounts the intellectual feud between Harry Jaffa and Walter Berns that proved to resemble the feud between Thomas Jefferson and John Adams. Through the story of those intellectuals (along with others), Hayward aims to explain why being patriotic to the United States shouldn't be a forced task.

McKenna, George. *The Puritan Origins of American Patriotism*. New Haven, CT: Yale University Press, 2007. In this book, George McKenna discusses the history of American patriotism, its protestant and puritan origin, and how the influence can be seen in present time.

Rothbard, Murray N. *The Progressive Era*. Auburn, AL: Ludwig von Mises Institute, 2017. This is a posthumous book by Murray N. Rothbard. It is about the Progressive Era (1896-1916), which still influences today's politics and economy. It talks about systemic racism, business monopoly, and American expansion abroad, which are at the center of the debate over patriotism.

Skeers, Linda. *The Impossible Patriotism Project (Rise and Shine)*. New York, NY: Puffin Books, 2009. This book offers a fictional take on patriotism. It depicts the story of Caleb, an army child.

Periodicals and Internet Sources

Bai, Matt. "Trump confuses nationalism with patriotism. We shouldn't," Yahoo News, May 30, 2019. https://news.yahoo.com/trump-confuses-nationalism-with-patriotism-we-shouldnt-090000852.html.

Ernst, Douglas. "Booker plans 'patriotism' pitch for voters who love Trump economy, oppose higher taxes," *Washington Times*, May 6, 2019. https://www.washingtontimes.com/news/2019/may/6/cory-booker-plans-patriotism-pitch-for-voters-who-/.

Fonte, John. "The virtues of patriotism," American Greatness, May 23, 2019. https://amgreatness.com/2019/05/23/the-virtues-of-patriotism/.

Galston, William A. "In defense of a reasonable patriotism," Brookings, June 25, 2018. https://www.brookings.edu/research/in-defense-of-a-reasonable-patriotism/.

Goldberg, Jonah. "Our strange relationship with the word 'patriotism,'" *Chicago Tribune,* July 6, 2018. https://www.chicagotribune.com/opinion/commentary/ct-perspec-goldberg-patriotism-nationalism-dissent-0709-20180706-story.html.

Keith's Blog. "The true meaning of patriotism," April 12, 2015. https://sites.psu.edu/eagles/2015/04/12/the-true-meaning-of-patriotism/.

McClay, Wilfred M. "How to think about patriotism," National Affairs, Spring 2018. https://www.nationalaffairs.com/publications/detail/how-to-think-about-patriotism.

Monteiro, Mariana. "What does patriotism mean when you're a citizen of two different countries?" Daily Universe, May 17, 2019. https://universe.byu.edu/2019/05/17/what-does-patriotism-mean-when-youre-a-citizen-of-two-different-countries-1/.

Serazio, Michael. "How empty displays of sports patriotism allow Americans to forget the troops," *Washington Post*, May 24,

2019. https://www.washingtonpost.com/outlook/2019/05/24/how-empty-displays-sports-patriotism-allow-americans-forget-troops/?noredirect=on&utm_term=.eedbe0c91458.

Shea, Daniel M. "A small act of patriotism," *Boston Globe*, May 27, 2019. https://www.bostonglobe.com/opinion/2019/05/27/small-act-patriotism/pSqIdF9WRNmbFXLFbY5ZUI/story.html.

Smith, Jeremy Adam. "Can patriotism be compassionate?" *Greater Good Magazine*, July 2, 2013. https://greatergood.berkeley.edu/article/item/can_patriotism_be_compassionate

Teichner, Martha. "How do you define patriotism?" *CBS News*, November 2, 2008. https://www.cbsnews.com/news/how-do-you-define-patriotism/.

Zarroli, Jim. "In Trump's trade war, Americans will be asked to show economic patriotism," NPR, May 20, 2019. https://www.npr.org/2019/05/20/724357301/in-trumps-trade-war-americans-will-be-asked-to-show-economic-patriotism.

Websites

The Foundation for Liberty and American Greatness (www.flagusa.org)
This nonprofit organization, founded in 2016, develops civic-education materials for students to help them build a patriotic lifestyle. It achieves its mission by providing complementary classroom presentations and bringing relevant guest speakers to schools.

The Heritage Foundation (www.heritage.org)
Founded in 1973, the Heritage Foundation is a research institution focused on promoting conservative public policies and ideas. By doing so, it hopes that freedom, prosperity, opportunity, and civil society are at the forefront of America's future.

National Foundation of Patriotism (www.foundationofpatriotism.org)
This organization aims to ensure that patriotism has a place in the life of every American. It believes that this is how the country can move forward and have a meaningful impact in the world.

Index

A

Abrams v. United States, 60
American Patriotism in a Global Society, 65
American Protective League (APL), 56, 58, 60

B

Ballet of the Nations, The, 37, 40
Beirich, Heidi, 95–102
Berns, Walter, 63, 65
Biden, Joe, 17, 21
Bin Laden, Osama, 13, 15
Bioshock: Infinite, 18
Bonaparte, Napoleon, 8, 33, 34
Bosché, Gabrielle, 74–77
Brandenburg v. Ohio, 60
Brooks, David, 25, 29–30, 32

C

Charleston church shooting, 8, 99
Chauvin, Nicholas, 8, 33–36
chauvinism, history of the term, 8, 10, 33–36
Chesterton, G. K., 16
civic engagement, as predictor of patriotism, 78–85
Clinton, Hillary, 13, 30
Costello, Carol, 20, 23
Craige, Betty Jean, 63, 65

D

Debs, Eugene V., 59–60
De Fina, Anna, 103–109
Democrats, and theories of patriotism, 86–89
Duina, Francesco, 68–72

E

Environmental Protection Agency (EPA), 46
Espionage Act, 56–61
ethnocentrism, 8

F

FIFA, 36
First Amendment, 57
flag burning, 9
Frankovic, Kathy, 86–89

G

globalists, compared to nationalists, 24–32
global patriotism, 43–48

H

Haidt, Jonathan, 24–32
Haiti, history of, 14–15, 16
Haitian people, massacre of in Dominican Republic, 8
Harmon, Marcel, 43–48
hate crimes, relation to nationalism, 95–102
Holocaust, 8

I

independence, importance of patriotism to, 49–54
Iraq War, 62–67
Islamic terrorism, 7, 25

J

jury duty, 8

K

Kaepernick, Colin, 9, 103–109
Khan, Humayun, 30–31
Khan, Khizr, 30
Kramer, Lloyd, 19–20, 21

L

Lee, Sheila Jackson, 20
Lipscomb, Todd, 21–22
"Love of Country," 49, 50, 52
Lumen Learning, 56–61

M

Made in USA Forever, 18, 22
mail, censorship of, 56, 58
"Make America Great Again" (MAGA) slogan, 7, 13
Marxism, 10, 90–94
McCann, Adam, 78–85
McCarthyism, 46
military enlistment, 9, 78–85
millennials, 74–77
Miller, David, 25, 29, 32
Monbiot, George, 25, 27, 32

N

national anthem, 9, 44, 46, 103–109

National Football League (NFL), 9, 103–109
nationalism, explanation of, 8, 17–23
nationalists, compared to globalists, 24–32
"New Chauvinism, The," 25, 27

O

Obama, Barack, 7, 20, 21, 88, 89
Office of Government Ethics, 46
Olympics, 44
Ostrom, Elinor, 46, 47

P

Paget, Violet (Vernon Lee), 37–41
Palin, Sarah, 17, 20
Parsley massacre, 8
patriotism, explanation of, 8
Pearl Harbor, 25
Perry, Rick, 17, 20
Philippines, struggle for independence in, 49–54
Pledge of Allegiance, 9
poverty, and patriotism in the United States, 68–72
presidential election of 2016, 12–16
Pulham, Patricia, 37–41

Q

Quirk, Michael, 12–16

R

Rapinoe, Megan, 108
Republicans, and theories of patriotism, 86–89

Reyno, Ma. Cielito, 49–54
Rizal, Jose, 49–54
Rock, Chris, 9
Romney, Mitt, 17, 20
Roosevelt, Theodore, 58
Rutland, Peter, 21

S
Sagan, Carl, 36
Sanders, Bernie, 71
Sedition Act, 56–61
Selective Service, 46
September 11, 2001, terrorist
    attacks, 25
Sessions, Jeff, 95, 100–101
Solo, Hope, 36
Spanish-American War, 52
sports, and patriotism,
    44, 103–109
Summers, Larry, 28
Sunkara, Bhaskar, 90–94

T
taxes, 8, 21, 43, 78
Trump, Donald, 7, 8, 13, 24,
    28, 30, 31, 43, 46, 47, 48,
    71, 88, 89, 95, 96–97, 99,
    100, 102, 106, 108

U
*United States v. Motion Picture
    Film*, 60
US Supreme Court, 9, 60

V
voting, 8, 46, 79, 84

W
war, importance of patriotism
    during, 37–41
Weeks, Linton, 17–23
white supremacists, 8, 95–102
Wilton, Dave, 33–36
Wisniewski, Sharon, 62–67
World's Fair of 1939, 91
World War I, 36–41, 56–61
World War II, 40, 46, 90

Picture Credits

Cover Stephen J. Boitano/Lonely Planet Images/Getty Images; p. 11 Image Source/Getty Images; p. 14 Raleigh News & Observer/Tribune News Service/Getty Images; p. 19 Anton Gvozdikov/Shutterstock .com; p. 26 S. Borisov/Shutterstock.com; p. 35 De Agostini Picture Library/Getty Images; p. 39 The History Collection/Alamy Stock Photo; p. 42 Barbara Singer/Archive Photos/Getty Images; p. 45 goir/Shutterstockcom; p. 51 Gabriel Mistral/Getty Images; p. 59 Keystone-France/Gamma-Keystone/Getty Images; p. 64 Ariel Skelley/DigitalVision/Getty Images; pp. 70, 88 Mario Tama/Getty Images; p. 73 Mark Kanning/Alamy Stock Photo; p. 76 tommaso79/ Shutterstock.com; p. 81 Cory A. Ulrich/Shutterstock.com; p. 92 Wikimedia Commons/File:Karl Marx 001.jpg/PD; p. 96 Bettmann/ Getty Images; p. 105 Michael Zagaris/Getty Images.

Photo Researcher: Sherri Jackson